PICKLING AND FERMENTING FOR BEGINNERS

The Complete Step-by-Step Guide to Safely Make Sauerkraut, Kimchi, and Pickles and Master the Art of Home Fermentation

ANGELA ROWEN

GRAPEVINE BOOKS

Published by

GRAPEVINE BOOKS

www.grapevinebooks.com

email: contact@grapevinebooks.com

Ordering Information:

Quantity sales: Special discounts are available on quantity purchases
by corporations, associations, and others.
For details, reach out to the publisher.

First published by Grapevine Books, 2025

Contents

Introduction

Welcome to the World of Pickling and Fermenting

Congratulations on starting your journey into the world of pickling and fermenting! Whether you're interested in preserving your garden harvest, experimenting with new flavors, or simply enjoying the numerous health benefits that come from these methods, you're in the right place. Pickling and fermenting offer incredible versatility in the kitchen, allowing you to transform ordinary fruits, vegetables, and even proteins into something extraordinary. Not only do these techniques help you enjoy your favorite foods year-round, but they also allow you to develop unique flavors that store-bought options can't match.

With a little time and the right knowledge, you'll be able to create a wide variety of delicious and nutritious preserved foods. You'll discover the satisfaction of turning fresh ingredients into tangy pickles, probiotic-rich ferments, and a host of other delightful creations. The best part? It's a skill that grows with you as you experiment and perfect your techniques.

Why This Book is Essential for Your Food Preservation Journey

This book is your go-to guide for mastering the art of pickling and fermenting. Whether you're a complete beginner or someone with some experience, the easy-to-follow steps and expert tips within these pages will empower you to create vibrant, flavorful preserved foods. You'll learn all the essentials, from understanding the difference between pickling and fermenting to using the right tools and ingredients. Most importantly, this book will provide you with everything you need to build confidence and succeed in your food preservation journey.

By following along, you'll unlock the secrets behind making quick pickles, fermented vegetables, probiotic-rich beverages, and more. Each chapter is designed to break down the processes in clear, simple language, so you can learn at your own pace. You'll start with the basics and move towards more advanced techniques, gaining a deeper understanding of both the art and science of food preservation.

Overview of Pickling, Fermenting, and Gut Health Benefits

Pickling and fermenting do more than just preserve food, they enhance its flavors and offer a wealth of health benefits. By the end of this guide, you'll understand how each method works, the various types of food you can preserve, and how to tailor the strength and taste of your creations to match your personal preferences.

Fermented foods are particularly valuable due to their gut health benefits. These foods are packed with probiotics, the "good" bacteria that support digestion, boost immunity, and contribute to a healthy microbiome. Whether you're making sauerkraut, kimchi, kombucha, or other ferments, you'll be nurturing your gut health while enjoying some delicious flavors along the way.

Pickling, while not as focused on probiotics, offers its own unique set of benefits. Pickled vegetables and fruits are rich in antioxidants and can add bold, tangy flavors to your meals. The process of pickling allows you to preserve your favorite vegetables when they're out of season, giving you year-round access to delightful, zesty snacks and sides.

With each technique you explore in this book, you'll gain a better understanding of how these preservation methods can improve your diet, your health, and your cooking skills. So, let's get started on this exciting, flavorful journey of pickling and fermenting!

Chapter 1
Introduction to Pickling and Fermenting

What Is Pickling and Fermentation?

Have you ever wondered how foods like pickles, kimchi, and kombucha get their distinctive sour flavors? What makes them last so long in your pantry or fridge? The answer lies in two incredible food preservation methods: pickling and fermentation.

Pickling is a process that involves immersing vegetables, fruits, or meats in an acidic solution, typically made from vinegar, salt, and water. The food absorbs the brine, which alters its texture and imparts a sharp, tangy flavor, often accompanied by a crisp bite. The beauty of pickling lies in its simplicity and versatility; it is a process that can be used on a wide range of foods, from cucumbers and radishes to fruits like peaches and pears. The spices and seasonings added to the brine allow for endless flavor combinations, enabling the creation of pickles that suit individual tastes.

Fermentation, on the other hand, is a natural process driven by the activity of beneficial bacteria, yeast, or molds. These microorganisms break down the sugars present in food, producing organic acids, alcohols, and gases, which preserve the food and develop unique flavors. Fermented foods like kimchi, sauerkraut, kombucha, and yogurt are rich in probiotics, which are beneficial bacteria that promote a healthy gut. Unlike pickling, which relies on an external acidic solution, fermentation depends on the natural activity of microbes to create the acidic environment that preserves the food. The result is not just a preserved food item, but one that offers probiotic benefits and more complex, tangy flavors.

Choosing between pickling and fermentation depends largely on what you're looking for in terms of flavor and health benefits. Pickling is a quicker method that adds immediate tang and flavor to food, making it ideal for those who want a fast, easy preservation technique. Fermentation, while a slower process, offers health benefits such as gut health improvement and more complex flavor development, making it perfect for those interested in the long-term rewards of probiotics and deeper, more intricate tastes.

The Role of Salt in Pickling

Salt is one of the most essential ingredients in pickling, playing a crucial role in both the preservation and flavor development of pickled foods. It is often the primary ingredient in the brine, helping to draw out moisture from the vegetables and creating the right environment for pickling and fermentation to take place. This process, known as osmosis, allows the vegetables to release their water, which then combines with the salt to form a brine that helps preserve the food.

Beyond just flavor, salt also plays a protective role during the fermentation process. It helps to inhibit the growth of harmful bacteria and molds, ensuring that only beneficial bacteria, such as Lactobacillus, thrive. These beneficial bacteria are responsible for the fermentation process, turning sugars into lactic acid, which is what gives fermented pickles their signature tangy flavor. By controlling the amount of salt used, you can influence the rate of fermentation and the final taste of your pickles.

Different types of salt can be used in pickling, with pickling salt being the most commonly recommended. Pickling salt is pure sodium chloride without any additives like iodine or anti-caking agents, which can affect the clarity of the brine and the texture of the vegetables. Kosher salt and sea salt are also popular choices, though it's important to adjust the quantities when using these salts, as their grain sizes differ from pickling salt. Using the right type of salt ensures that the pickles will ferment correctly and develop the desired taste and texture.

Salt concentration is key to the pickling process. A too-low concentration might fail to preserve the food properly, while too much salt can make the pickles overly salty and inhibit fermentation. The optimal salt concentration typically ranges from 2-5% of the brine's total volume, depending on the type of vegetable being pickled and the desired result. Understanding how much salt to use and how it interacts with other ingredients is fundamental to achieving the perfect pickle.

Ultimately, salt not only enhances the flavor of pickles but also creates the right environment for the pickling and fermentation processes to occur, ensuring the preservation of the vegetables and the development of the tangy, probiotic-rich flavors that make pickled foods so special.

The Health Benefits of Probiotics and Preserved Foods

Fermented foods are more than just flavorful additions to your meals, they are a powerhouse of health benefits. The key lies in the probiotics they contain, live bacteria and yeasts that are essential for maintaining gut health. Probiotics help balance the microorganisms in your digestive tract, preventing harmful bacteria from taking hold while promoting the growth of beneficial microbes. These "good" bacteria are essential for digesting food, synthesizing vitamins, and enhancing the immune system.

Probiotics have been linked to improved digestive health, especially for conditions like irritable bowel syndrome (IBS), bloating, and constipation. But the benefits don't end there; they also play a role in mental health by influencing the gut-brain axis, a communication pathway between your digestive system and brain. For example, kimchi, sauerkraut, kefir, and kombucha are all excellent sources of probiotics that can help enhance digestion and boost immunity. By regularly consuming these probiotic-rich foods, you can support a balanced microbiome, which is essential for overall health.

While fermented foods pack the biggest punch in terms of probiotics, pickled foods still offer significant health benefits. Though vinegar-based pickles do not provide probiotics, they offer antioxidants that protect cells from oxidative stress. Pickled vegetables retain many of the nutrients of their fresh counterparts, including vitamins and minerals. The vinegar used in the brine also offers health benefits, such as helping to regulate blood sugar levels and promoting healthy digestion. While pickles may not be a source of probiotics, they still add nutritional value to your diet and contribute to a well-rounded, health-conscious lifestyle.

So, whether you lean towards fermented foods for their probiotic benefits or pickled foods for their vibrant flavors and nutritional value, both have a place in a healthy diet. You don't have to choose one, enjoy both, creating a balanced approach to food preservation that caters to your taste and health needs.

Pickling for Seasonal Harvests

One of the best things about pickling is its ability to preserve seasonal produce and make it last throughout the year. Whether you have an overflowing garden or find great deals at your local farmer's market, pickling offers a way to capture the flavors of the season and enjoy them long after the produce is no longer in season. Seasonal vegetables and fruits are often at their peak in terms of flavor and nutritional content, making them ideal candidates for pickling.

For example, summer vegetables like cucumbers, zucchini, and peppers can be pickled and enjoyed all year. Tomatoes and green beans are other vegetables that lend themselves well to pickling during their peak harvest time. Autumn produce like apples, pears, and pumpkins can also be preserved through pickling. Fruits such as apples and peaches are particularly good for sweet pickling, giving you a way to enjoy their natural sweetness, even after the season is over.

Spring and fall are particularly important seasons for pickling. These are the times when you can find a wide variety of produce in abundance, things like radishes, carrots, and cauliflower during the spring, and brussels sprouts, beets, and turnips during the fall. These vegetables are perfect candidates for pickling, as they tend to be hearty and hold up well in brine, retaining their crunch and flavor throughout the year.

While you might associate pickling primarily with vegetables, fruits also make excellent pickles, especially when they are in season. Stone fruits, like peaches, plums, and cherries, offer a unique sweetness when pickled and can add a refreshing contrast to your usual pickled vegetables. Berries like raspberries, blackberries, and strawberries are also great for pickling and can be used in both savory and sweet applications.

What's wonderful about seasonal pickling is that it allows you to extend the shelf life of fruits and vegetables, enabling you to enjoy summer's bounty even in the winter months. With a bit of creativity, you can mix different vegetables and fruits together, experimenting with different flavors and textures to create unique and personalized pickles.

The History and Tradition of Pickling and Fermenting

Pickling and fermenting are not modern inventions; they have been practiced for thousands of years, offering a way to preserve food and enhance its flavor long before refrigeration and canning were available. The practice of pickling dates back to around 2400 BCE in ancient Mesopotamia, where cucumbers were first pickled in brine. This method of food preservation spread across the globe, as civilizations recognized the necessity of preserving food for times when fresh produce was not readily available.

The Egyptians were among the first to embrace pickles as a food staple, using them for long voyages to prevent scurvy. The Romans were no strangers to pickles either, and they believed pickles helped boost the strength of soldiers. Fermentation, another ancient preservation method, was equally important. In many cultures, it was used not just to preserve food but also to enhance its nutritional value. Ancient records suggest that the Chinese were fermenting foods like soybeans to create early versions of miso, while Korean cuisine has been deeply shaped by the art of fermenting, with kimchi being a central feature of the diet.

Throughout Europe, fermentation and pickling became integral parts of food culture. In Eastern Europe, particularly in countries like Germany and Poland, fermented cabbage became a staple, leading to the beloved sauerkraut that we still enjoy today. In Russia, fermented dairy products like kefir and yogurt were commonplace, providing essential nutrients during the long winters. In fact, the art of fermenting was often passed down through generations as a treasured tradition.

As global trade and exploration increased, the practice of pickling and fermenting spread to every corner of the world. What began as a necessity for survival eventually evolved into a culinary tradition that celebrates both flavors and cultural heritage. By embracing these time-honored techniques, you're connecting with thousands of years of human history and joining in the global tradition of preserving food for future enjoyment.

The Importance of Proper Storage

Once your pickles or fermented foods are ready, proper **storage** is essential to maintaining their quality, flavor, and safety. The way you store your pickled or fermented foods can greatly affect their shelf life and overall taste. Three factors are crucial in preserving the integrity of your food: temperature, light, and air exposure.

Temperature plays a significant role in the rate at which fermentation or pickling continues. For fermented foods, once the fermentation process is complete and you've reached the desired flavor, it's important to store them in a cool environment, such as a refrigerator. Cold temperatures slow down the fermentation process, allowing the food to maintain its flavor and texture for an extended period. If left at room temperature too long, fermented foods can continue fermenting and become overly sour or mushy.

For pickled foods, the temperature is less critical once they've been processed and sealed in jars. However, it's still best to store pickles in a cool, dark place, such as a pantry or cupboard, to avoid exposing them to sunlight, which can cause the pickles to degrade more quickly. Once opened, however, pickles should be refrigerated to maintain their crispness and flavor.

Light exposure can also have an adverse effect on pickles and fermented foods. Direct sunlight can degrade the quality of the brine, especially for lighter-colored pickles. In particular, if you use vinegar-based pickles, they should be stored away from light to prevent them from becoming discolored and losing their vibrant color. Fermented foods, such as kombucha or kimchi, should also be kept away from bright light, which can affect the fermentation process.

Air exposure is another important factor. Oxygen can introduce mold, yeast, or other contaminants into the jar, spoiling the food. This is especially important for fermented foods, which require a controlled environment to thrive. Using an airlock system or sealed jar lids will help keep oxygen out, allowing beneficial bacteria to flourish without interference from harmful microorganisms. Pickles in brine are generally safe from oxygen exposure if sealed correctly, but once opened, they should be refrigerated and consumed within a reasonable timeframe.

By understanding these storage guidelines, you can extend the shelf life of your pickles and ferments while maintaining their texture and taste. Proper storage ensures that you can enjoy the fruits of your labor for months and even years, making the most of your efforts and preserving the health benefits.

Understanding Lacto-Fermentation vs. Vinegar-Based Pickling

When it comes to preserving food, lacto-fermentation and vinegar-based pickling are two of the most popular methods. But what sets them apart, and how do these processes work?

Lacto-fermentation relies on the action of naturally occurring bacteria, particularly Lactobacillus, to convert the sugars in vegetables into lactic acid. This creates the acidic environment that preserves the food and gives it its characteristic tangy flavor. The beauty of lacto-fermentation lies in the fact that it also produces probiotics, the beneficial bacteria that promote gut health. Foods such as kimchi, sauerkraut, and fermented pickles are made through this process. While lacto-fermentation takes longer to complete, usually from a few days to several weeks, it results in a probiotic-rich food that's not only preserved but also beneficial for your digestive system.

On the other hand, vinegar-based pickling uses an acidic brine, typically composed of vinegar, salt, and sometimes sugar. The food is submerged in this brine and, through the acid, is preserved quickly, often within a few hours or days. This method does not introduce probiotics into the food, but the vinegar itself acts as a preservative, creating a tangy, sharp flavor. Vinegar-based pickles, such as those made with cucumbers or onions, are ready in a much shorter time and are perfect for those looking for immediate results.

The major difference between these two methods lies in the time required and the health benefits. Lacto-fermentation takes longer but offers the added benefit of probiotics, which support gut health. Vinegar-based pickling is faster, providing a quicker way to enjoy pickled foods, but it lacks the probiotic content. Depending on your needs, whether you're seeking an immediate flavorful snack or a more complex, health-promoting food, both methods have their place in your kitchen.

Understanding pH and Acidity in Fermentation and Pickling

When it comes to both pickling and fermentation, pH and acidity play a pivotal role in determining the success of the preservation process and the safety of the final product. pH measures the acidity or alkalinity of a substance, with lower pH levels indicating higher acidity. In pickling, achieving the correct pH is essential for preventing the growth of harmful bacteria and ensuring that the food stays safe to consume. For a pickle to be safe and properly preserved, the pH of the brine or the fermenting environment needs to fall within the range of 3.4 to 3.6. This level of acidity prevents harmful pathogens from flourishing while allowing beneficial bacteria to do their work.

In lacto-fermentation, the naturally occurring bacteria, such as Lactobacillus, convert sugars into lactic acid, which lowers the pH of the ferment and gives it that characteristic tangy flavor. The process of fermentation gradually decreases the pH, and once it reaches the desired level, the food is preserved, and the beneficial bacteria flourish. For vinegar-based pickling, the pH is controlled externally by adding vinegar (acetic acid) to the brine, which immediately lowers the pH and helps preserve the food. In this method, it's crucial to use the right vinegar, as vinegars can vary in acidity. For pickling purposes, you should always aim for vinegar with an acidity of 5% or higher.

Measuring pH during pickling and fermentation is vital for ensuring safety. Using a pH meter or pH test strips can help you monitor the acidity throughout the process, making sure the food remains within the safe range. When fermenting at home, you can also rely on visual and sensory cues, like the presence of bubbles (for fermentation) or the right balance of tartness and flavor, to gauge progress. However, for the safest and most consistent results, especially when scaling up or experimenting with more complex recipes, using a pH meter is recommended.

This section would help readers understand how to monitor and adjust acidity levels, ensuring that the pickling or fermenting process is not only flavorful but safe.

Chapter 2
Getting Started with Pickling

Essential Tools and Equipment for Pickling

When it comes to pickling, the right tools can make all the difference in achieving the perfect jar of pickles. At the most basic level, pickling doesn't require many specialized tools, but having the right equipment can ensure that the process goes smoothly and your pickles turn out just the way you want them. First and foremost, mason jars are a must. These jars are specifically designed for canning and are available in various sizes, but for most pickling recipes, quart or pint-sized jars work best. Be sure to use new lids to ensure a proper seal, as old lids may not function effectively.

For preparing the brine, you'll need a large pot that can hold the brine and vegetables comfortably. A non-reactive pot, such as one made of stainless steel, enamel, or ceramic, is essential since acidic ingredients like vinegar can react with certain metals, affecting the flavor and safety of the pickles. Additionally, a ladle will help you fill the jars without spilling, while a funnel will ensure that the brine doesn't spill over the sides of the jar. If you plan to ferment your vegetables, you'll need a fermentation weight to keep your veggies submerged under the brine, preventing exposure to air, which could lead to mold growth.

When you begin canning, you'll also need a canner or large stockpot for the water bath process, which ensures that the jars are sealed tightly. Using a jar lifter to handle hot jars is crucial for safety, and a clean cloth to wipe the rims of the jars before sealing them is equally important to ensure a perfect seal. While these tools are essential, the beauty of pickling is that you don't need to invest in a lot of specialized equipment right away, especially for beginners. You can start with simple items you already have in your kitchen and gradually build your collection as you become more confident in the pickling process.

Choosing Ingredients for Pickling Success

What makes a pickle truly special? The ingredients! While the pickling process itself is relatively simple, the key to achieving the best pickles lies in selecting high-quality vegetables, spices, and liquids. By carefully choosing your ingredients, you can elevate the taste and texture of your pickles and ensure they turn out delicious every time.

Fresh, High-Quality Produce

For the best pickles, start with fresh, in-season vegetables. The quality of the product directly affects the final outcome. Cucumbers, carrots, cauliflower, green beans, and even fruits like peaches or pears make for excellent pickling choices. Select firm, blemish-free produce with no soft spots, as this ensures the pickles will remain crisp. Fresh vegetables not only provide better texture but also offer vibrant flavor. If you're harvesting from your garden, the early morning hours are ideal for picking, as this is when vegetables are freshest and full of moisture. If you're purchasing from the market, choose local, in-season produce for the best flavor and cost-effectiveness.

Salt

Salt plays an essential role in both the preservation and flavor development of pickles. Always choose pickling salt, which is free from additives like iodine. Iodine can cause the brine to turn cloudy and can negatively affect the flavor of the pickles. Pickling salt is finely granulated and dissolves easily, ensuring that your brine remains clean and clear, resulting in the perfect pickle every time. Avoid regular table salt, as it may contain anti-caking agents that could affect the clarity and texture of your pickles.

Vinegar

Vinegar is the acidic solution that gives pickles their characteristic tang, making them safe to eat while preserving them. Distilled white vinegar and apple cider vinegar are the most commonly used vinegars for pickling, each contributing a distinct flavor. Apple cider vinegar is milder and slightly sweeter, with more complexity, which pairs well with sweeter pickles or those requiring a more rounded flavor. White vinegar, on the other hand, has a sharper, more pronounced acidity, making it perfect for crisp pickles where a clean, tart bite is desired. When choosing vinegar for your pickling recipes, it's important to use vinegar with at least 5% acidity to ensure proper preservation.

Spices and Seasonings

The spices and seasonings you choose are what truly set your pickles apart. While mustard seeds, dill, coriander, peppercorns, garlic, bay leaves, and red pepper flakes are common ingredients for classic pickling brines, don't be afraid to get creative with your spice choices. Experiment with turmeric to add a warm, golden hue and a subtle earthiness, or thyme for a fragrant, savory twist. Cumin and cloves can introduce a deeper, spicier note to your pickles, while fresh herbs like rosemary or basil can infuse your pickles with a refreshing, aromatic quality. The key to creating pickles that reflect your tastes is finding the right balance of spices that complement the vegetables you are using.

Water

Water is the unsung hero in the pickling process. It's important to use filtered water when making your brine. Tap water often contains chlorine and other minerals that can interfere with the flavor of your pickles. If you don't have access to filtered water, simply let the tap water sit for a few hours to allow the chlorine to dissipate. This simple step ensures that your brine remains pure and clean-tasting, allowing the flavors of your vegetables and spices to shine.

Seasonal and Local Produce

For those looking to make pickling a more sustainable practice, consider focusing on seasonal and local produce. Not only does this reduce the environmental impact of transportation, but it also allows you to take advantage of fruits and vegetables at their peak flavor and ripeness. Whether you're pickling in the summer with an abundance of cucumbers and peppers or preserving the flavors of fall with apples and pears, working with seasonal produce ensures that your pickles are as fresh and flavorful as possible.

By focusing on these key ingredients and selecting them with care, you'll be well on your way to creating the perfect pickles. Whether you're a beginner or an experienced pickler, the foundation for great pickles lies in choosing the right vegetables, spices, and liquids. With this knowledge, you'll be able to create pickles that not only preserve your favorite foods but also add vibrant, bold flavors to your meals.

Step-by-Step Guide to Basic Pickling

Ready to start pickling? Here's a simple, foolproof guide to get you going. Pickling is one of the easiest ways to preserve vegetables, and with this basic recipe, you'll be able to make tangy, flavorful pickles in no time.

1. Prepare the Vegetables

Start by washing your vegetables thoroughly. Cut them to the desired size, whether that's slicing cucumbers into spears, cutting carrots into sticks, or leaving small vegetables like green beans whole. Make sure the pieces fit comfortably into the mason jars you'll be using. For cucumbers, removing the ends can help them stay crisp.

2. Make the Brine

In a large pot, combine your vinegar, water, and salt (use the ratio of 1 part vinegar, 1 part water, and 1–2 tablespoons of salt per jar). Bring it to a boil, stirring until the salt is dissolved. You can also add sugar if you prefer a sweeter brine. Add your spices to the brine at this point garlic, dill, mustard seeds, or any spices you like.

3. Pack the Jars

Once the brine is boiling, remove it from the heat. Carefully pack your vegetables into the mason jars. You can tightly pack them to make sure they're all submerged, but leave about half an inch of space at the top for the brine to expand. If you're using pickling weights, place them on top of the vegetables.

4. Pour the Brine

Using a ladle or measuring cup, pour the hot brine over the vegetables in each jar. Be sure the vegetables are fully submerged, and wipe the rim of each jar with a clean towel before sealing. If necessary, add more brine to fill the jar completely.

5. Seal and Store

Place the lids on the jars and screw them on tightly. Let the jars cool to room temperature before placing them in the refrigerator. If you're canning your pickles, you'll need to process the jars in a water bath. Otherwise, your pickles should be ready to enjoy within a few days!

6. Let the Pickles Rest

For the best flavor, let your pickles sit in the fridge for at least 48 hours. Some pickles will develop more complex flavors as they age, so the longer you wait, the better they may taste.

Common Mistakes to Avoid

While pickling may seem like a simple task, there are a few common pitfalls that can result in less-than-ideal pickles. One of the most frequent mistakes is not properly sterilizing your jars. Failing to do so can introduce harmful bacteria into your pickles, leading to spoilage. Always ensure that your jars and lids are properly sanitized before use. This can be done by boiling them for 10-15 minutes or running them through a dishwasher on the hottest setting.

Another common error is overpacking the jars. Vegetables need room to expand and release gases during fermentation, so avoid tightly packing them in the jar. Too much pressure on the vegetables can lead to broken jars or an uneven fermentation process. Similarly, underpacking or leaving too much air space can cause the vegetables to float above the brine, exposing them to oxygen and inviting mold growth.

It's also crucial not to skip the pH checks if you are using vinegar for pickling. The acidity of the brine should always fall within a safe range to prevent bacterial growth. Testing the pH with strips or a meter can help ensure your pickles are safe.

Finally, be patient. Pickles and fermented foods need time to develop their flavors fully. It's tempting to open a jar early, but the best pickles often require several days or even weeks to achieve their optimal flavor. Over time, the brine will marry with the vegetables, and the flavors will deepen, giving you that perfect balance of tang and crunch.

The Role of Sugar in Pickling

Sugar is often seen as an optional ingredient in pickling, but it plays a vital role in the overall process, both in terms of flavor and fermentation. When used in pickling, sugar balances out the acidity of the vinegar, providing a subtle sweetness that can help round out the tangy, salty flavors in the brine. It works alongside salt to create the ideal conditions for pickling vegetables and fruits, ensuring that the flavors are both rich and well-rounded.

One of the most important functions of sugar in the pickling process is its ability to promote fermentation. When pickling vegetables or fruits through a fermentation process, sugar acts as the food source for beneficial bacteria like Lactobacillus. These bacteria feed on the sugars, turning them into lactic acid, which is the key element that gives fermented pickles their characteristic tang. Without sugar, fermentation might not proceed effectively, and the pickles may not develop the desired flavor or texture.

In addition to its role in fermentation, sugar also helps with preservation. While vinegar is the primary preservative in pickles, sugar can enhance the overall preservation process by contributing to the creation of a stable brine. A sweetened brine also creates a thicker liquid, which helps vegetables maintain their texture and remain crunchy throughout the pickling process. This is especially important when pickling fruits or vegetables with high water content, like cucumbers or peppers, as it helps them retain their firmness.

However, the amount of sugar used in pickling should be carefully considered. Too much sugar can result in pickles that are overly sweet and can overwhelm the acidity of the brine, while too little may fail to balance the sharpness of the vinegar and salt. Typically, pickling recipes will call for a moderate amount of sugar, which helps maintain the brine's effectiveness without dominating the taste. For example, many classic pickles, such as bread-and-butter pickles, rely on sugar to achieve their signature sweet-tangy balance.

In some cases, sugar can also be substituted with alternatives like honey, maple syrup, or coconut sugar, depending on dietary preferences or flavor profiles. These alternatives provide similar sweetness but with different undertones, allowing for more customization in your pickling process. Keep in mind, though, that using substitutes may slightly alter the final texture or color of the pickles, so it's important to experiment to find the best fit for your taste.

Ultimately, sugar in pickling serves a multifaceted purpose, from balancing acidity and enhancing fermentation to contributing to the preservation and texture of the final product. Whether you're pickling vegetables for quick use or fermenting them for long-term storage, understanding how sugar interacts with the brine and fermentation process is crucial to creating perfectly pickled food.

Chapter 3
Pickling Techniques and Recipes for Beginners

Whether you're new to pickling or have a bit of experience, understanding the basics of pickling techniques is essential for ensuring your efforts lead to delicious results. In this chapter, we're going to break down the techniques that will help you create the perfect pickles, from the simplest vinegar-based varieties to the more involved brining methods.

Pickling Techniques

Brining Pickles: A Classic Approach to Preservation

Brining is one of the most traditional and well-loved methods for pickling vegetables. It involves soaking vegetables in a saltwater solution, allowing natural bacteria to thrive and ferment the food. This method has been used for centuries to preserve the harvest and maintain food supplies throughout the year, long before refrigeration and modern preservation techniques were available. The beauty of brining lies in its simplicity and the depth of flavor it creates. While it may take a little longer than other methods, the end result is worth the wait, yielding pickles that are tangy, crunchy, and full of character.

How Brining Works

Brining works through the process of fermentation, where the salt in the brine draws out the moisture from the vegetables, creating a rich, flavorful brine that is both acidic and preservative. The brine becomes an ideal environment for beneficial bacteria to thrive, primarily lactic acid bacteria. These bacteria naturally convert sugars in the vegetables into lactic acid, which is what gives the pickles their signature sour taste and preserves them over time.

The fermentation process begins once the vegetables are submerged in the brine. The lactic acid bacteria multiply, producing lactic acid, which eventually lowers the pH of the brine, creating an acidic environment that protects the food from spoilage. This process can take anywhere from several days to a couple of weeks, depending on the temperature, type of vegetables used, and your personal taste preferences.

The Brining Process: Step-by-Step

The brining process starts with preparing the vegetables. The vegetables must be fresh and firm, with no signs of ripeness or soft spots, as they will be the base of your pickles. Popular vegetables for brining include cucumbers, green beans, carrots, cauliflower, and beets, but you can pickle almost any vegetable or fruit using this technique.

To begin, the vegetables are either whole or cut into desired shapes, depending on the recipe. After that, they are packed into a sterilized jar, ensuring they fit snugly. The next step is to prepare the brine, which typically consists of water, salt, and optionally, spices such as garlic, mustard seeds, dill, peppercorns, or bay leaves. Some recipes may also include a small amount of sugar to balance out the acidity.

Once the brine is made, it's poured over the vegetables, completely submerging them. If needed, you can use a weight to ensure that the vegetables stay submerged beneath the brine, as exposure to air can cause spoilage. After sealing the jar, it's left to ferment at room temperature. During this time, the beneficial bacteria get to work, fermenting the vegetables and creating the tangy brine.

How to Monitor the Brining Process

Unlike quicker pickling methods, brining takes time and patience. The process is mostly hands-off, but it's essential to monitor the jars during fermentation. Temperature plays a crucial role in how quickly your pickles ferment. In warmer temperatures (around 70°F to 75°F), fermentation can happen more quickly, while cooler temperatures will slow the process. It's important to keep your brine in a relatively consistent, cool area to prevent over-fermentation, which can make your pickles too soft or overly sour.

You can start tasting your pickles after about 4-5 days. As the fermentation progresses, the flavor will become tangier and more developed. If the brine becomes too sour, you can stop the fermentation by transferring the pickles to the fridge, which slows down the fermentation process.

Tips for Successful Brining

For successful brining, start with fresh, firm vegetables. Choose produce that is in-season and free from blemishes or soft spots. Fresh vegetables will provide the best texture and flavor for your pickles.

The salt concentration in your brine is key. Too little salt can lead to spoilage, while too much can prevent proper fermentation. A brine should contain 2-5% salt to water by weight, depending on the vegetables you are pickling.

It's crucial to keep your vegetables fully submerged in the brine. Exposure to air can cause spoilage, so use a weight or makeshift lid to keep them under the liquid. This helps create the right environment for fermentation.

Tasting your pickles as they ferment is a fun way to monitor the flavor. After a few days, taste your pickles and decide when they've reached the level of tanginess you prefer.

Finally, watch the temperature. Too high a temperature can over-ferment the pickles, while too low can slow down or stop the fermentation process. Keep your pickles in a cool, consistent spot for best results.

Troubleshooting Common Brining Issues

While brining is a relatively simple process, a few issues may arise during fermentation:

Cloudy Brine: This can occur if you use iodized salt, which should be avoided. Always use pickling salt, which dissolves easily and doesn't affect the clarity of the brine.

Soft Pickles: If your pickles turn out too soft, it could be due to using overripe vegetables or not soaking them in ice water long enough. Be sure to use firm, fresh vegetables and consider soaking them briefly in ice water to help them stay crisp.

Excessive Sourness: If the pickles become too sour for your taste, you can stop the fermentation by placing the jar in the refrigerator. This will slow down the process and preserve the flavor you desire.

When to Enjoy Your Brined Pickles

Brined pickles typically take 1-2 weeks to fully develop, depending on the temperature and your flavor preferences. Once they've reached the desired tanginess, transfer them to the refrigerator to halt further fermentation. Brined pickles can be stored for several months in the fridge, retaining their crispness and flavor.

Brining is an excellent way to preserve the vibrant flavors of fresh vegetables while adding a tangy, probiotic-rich punch to your meals. Whether you're making classic cucumber pickles or experimenting with carrots, cauliflower, or beets, brining offers a straightforward and reliable method for creating homemade pickles that will last long after the growing season ends.

Vinegar-Based Pickling: Quick and Simple

Vinegar-based pickling is one of the most common methods for beginners, as it's simple, quick, and doesn't require much time or specialized knowledge. This process involves soaking vegetables in an acidic solution made from vinegar, water, salt, and sugar. It's a fast and efficient way to create pickles that are tangy, flavorful, and ready to eat in a short amount of time, usually within a few hours to a couple of days.

The Basics of Vinegar-Based Pickling

Vinegar-based pickling relies on the sharp acidity of vinegar to preserve food. The most commonly used vinegars for this method are white distilled vinegar and apple cider vinegar, but other types of vinegar, such as rice vinegar or malt vinegar, can be used depending on the flavor profile you want to achieve. The vinegar's acidity is what prevents harmful bacteria from growing and keeps your vegetables safe for consumption.

Unlike fermented pickles, which rely on the natural bacteria present in vegetables to create an acidic environment, vinegar-based pickles are immediately acidic because the vinegar is added directly to the brine. This allows for much faster processing, which is why vinegar-based pickling is often the method of choice for those looking to preserve vegetables quickly or when the goal is to get pickles ready in a short amount of time.

How Vinegar-Based Pickling Works

The process is relatively simple. Vegetables are first prepared by cutting them into the desired shape whether slices, spears, or whole, depending on the type of vegetable and your preferences. The prepared vegetables are then packed tightly into sterilized jars. The brine, typically made of a mixture of vinegar, water, salt, and sugar, is brought to a boil to help dissolve the salt and sugar, then poured over the vegetables. The jars are sealed, and the pickles are allowed to sit at room temperature for a few hours to a couple of days.

While vinegar-based pickles are often associated with quick pickles, the pickles can still be stored in the refrigerator for months, allowing the flavors to develop further. However, they are usually not as tangy or complex as fermented pickles, which benefit from longer fermentation periods.

Common Vinegar-Based Pickling Liquids

The choice of vinegar plays a huge role in the final flavor of your pickles. White distilled vinegar is the most common vinegar used for pickling because of its sharp acidity and neutral flavor. This vinegar provides a clean, crisp flavor that allows the vegetables' natural flavors to shine. Apple cider vinegar, on the other hand, has a milder acidity and a slightly fruity taste, which works particularly well for pickling sweet vegetables like onions, carrots, or beets. Rice vinegar is a gentler vinegar that can be used for a sweeter pickle, perfect for pickling fruits like peaches or pears.

When making your brine, the general ratio for vinegar-based pickling is 1 part vinegar to 1 part water, with salt and sugar added to taste. Pickling salt is preferred because it dissolves easily and doesn't leave behind cloudy residue, which can occur with regular salt. Sugar is usually added to balance out the sharpness of the vinegar, with the amount depending on personal preference.

The Importance of Brine Proportions

The right balance of salt, sugar, and vinegar is crucial when making pickles. Too little salt and sugar will result in a bland brine, while too much can overpower the vegetables, making the pickles too salty or too sweet. The ideal brine ratio typically involves equal parts of vinegar and water, with the addition of salt and sugar in varying amounts based on the type of vegetables being pickled. Always remember to taste your brine before pouring it over your vegetables to ensure the flavor is balanced to your liking.

Tips for Successful Vinegar-Based Pickling

For successful vinegar-based pickling, always start with fresh, firm vegetables. Overripe or soft produce may not hold up well in the brine, potentially resulting in mushy pickles. Choose vegetables at their peak for the best texture and flavor, ensuring your pickles turn out crisp and delicious.

Sterilizing your jars is another crucial step. Clean and sterilize your jars thoroughly before filling them with vegetables and brine. This helps eliminate unwanted bacteria or contaminants, reducing the risk of spoilage or mold growth during the pickling process.

Experimenting with spices, herbs, and aromatics can elevate your pickles. While the basic brine consists of vinegar, water, salt, and sugar, adding ingredients like garlic, dill, mustard seeds, peppercorns, coriander, and chili flakes can give your pickles a unique flavor. These additions can transform simple pickles into a zesty condiment for various dishes.

Even though vinegar-based pickles can be eaten quickly, it's best to let them sit in the refrigerator for a couple of days before consuming. This allows the pickles to absorb the brine and develop a tangier flavor over time. The longer they sit, the more flavorful they become, so patience is key.

For storage, vinegar-based pickles should be kept in the refrigerator, where they will stay fresh for several months. For long-term storage, you can process the jars in a water bath canner to create a vacuum seal, allowing you to store your pickles in the pantry for up to a year. This makes them perfect for enjoying all year long.

When to Enjoy Vinegar-Based Pickles

One of the greatest benefits of vinegar-based pickles is how quickly they are ready. You can enjoy your pickles within a few hours to a couple of days. The flavor will intensify the longer they sit, so feel free to let them sit in the fridge for up to a week to develop more tang. Unlike fermented pickles, which may take a few weeks to reach their peak, vinegar-based pickles offer immediate gratification with that classic tart, tangy flavor.

Whether you're using quick pickling to preserve a bounty of seasonal vegetables or making them as a fun side dish for an evening meal, vinegar-based pickles are an easy, rewarding way to bring a burst of flavor to your meals. Their speed, simplicity, and versatility make them a perfect starting point for beginners looking to experiment with pickling.

Fermented Pickles: A Deeper, Probiotic Process

Fermented pickles are a step up from the basic vinegar-based pickles, offering a more complex and tangy flavor profile while providing an added health benefit: probiotics. Unlike vinegar-based pickles, which rely on an acidic brine to preserve the vegetables, fermented pickles depend on the natural process of fermentation, where beneficial bacteria break down sugars and turn them into lactic acid. This not only preserves the vegetables but also enhances their nutritional value.

The Basics of Fermented Pickles

Fermentation is an ancient preservation method that has been used for centuries to preserve foods like vegetables, dairy, and even meats. For pickles, the process is initiated by soaking vegetables in a saltwater brine. The key to successful fermentation is creating an environment where lactic acid bacteria (LAB) can thrive. These beneficial bacteria naturally occur on the surface of most vegetables and begin working as soon as they are submerged in the brine. As the bacteria feed on sugars, they produce lactic acid, which preserves the vegetables and gives them their characteristic tangy flavor.

Fermented pickles are not just tangy, they are also rich in probiotics, which are live beneficial bacteria that contribute to gut health. Probiotics help maintain a healthy balance of microorganisms in the gut, improving digestion, boosting immunity, and even supporting mental health. Unlike pickles made with vinegar, fermented pickles undergo a slow process of natural fermentation that allows the development of these beneficial bacteria.

How the Fermentation Process Works

To make fermented pickles, you'll need to create a saltwater brine, typically made with water and pickling salt. The salt helps to draw water out of the vegetables, creating a brine where the bacteria can thrive while also helping to keep out unwanted, spoilage-causing microorganisms. It's important to use non-iodized salt like pickling or kosher salt because iodine can inhibit fermentation and cloud the brine.

Once your brine is ready, pack your vegetables tightly into a clean jar, ensuring they are fully submerged in the brine. Vegetables like cucumbers, carrots, and cabbage (for sauerkraut) work well for fermentation, but you can experiment with other vegetables such as beets, radishes, and cauliflower.

The key to successful fermentation is to make sure that the vegetables remain submerged under the brine. You can achieve this by using a weight, a clean rock, or even a specialized fermentation weight. This ensures that the vegetables stay submerged and minimizes exposure to oxygen, which can lead to mold or spoilage.

The jar should then be placed in a warm, dark environment where it can ferment at a stable temperature. 68°F to 72°F (20°C to 22°C) is the ideal range for fermentation. After a few days, you will begin to notice bubbles forming in the brine, which is a sign that the bacteria are active and the fermentation process is underway. The length of fermentation varies depending on the temperature and the type of vegetable, but typically, fermentation can take anywhere from 3 days to a week.

Monitoring and Troubleshooting the Fermentation Process

While fermenting, it's important to check your pickles every few days to ensure they're developing correctly. You should notice the brine becoming cloudier as the fermentation progresses. The vegetables will also start to soften, and their flavor will become more tangy and complex. The fermentation process slows down once the vegetables are fully submerged in lactic acid and other metabolites produced by the bacteria.

If at any point you notice mold or scum on the surface of the brine, simply remove it with a clean spoon. This can sometimes happen when vegetables rise above the brine. However, do not taste or eat pickles with visible mold as it could indicate contamination.

Once your pickles have reached the level of sourness and texture you desire, remove the jar from the warm environment and transfer it to the refrigerator. The cooler temperature will slow the fermentation process and help preserve the probiotics and the pickle's flavor.

The Flavor Profile of Fermented Pickles

One of the most unique aspects of fermented pickles is the depth of flavor that develops over time. Unlike vinegar-based pickles, which offer a sharper, more immediate tang, fermented pickles offer a subtler sourness that comes from the lactic acid produced by the bacteria. The flavor will change over time as the pickles ferment further, becoming more complex and often more sour the longer they ferment. If you prefer a milder pickle, you can consume them after just a few days, but if you enjoy a more robust flavor, you can let them sit for a week or longer.

The texture of fermented pickles is also different. While vinegar-based pickles maintain their crisp texture, fermented pickles tend to soften a bit more, especially as they ferment. The long fermentation process allows the beneficial bacteria to break down the fibrous tissue in the vegetables, creating a tangier, more flavorful experience.

Benefits of Fermented Pickles

Fermented pickles offer a host of health benefits, primarily due to the probiotics they contain. These beneficial bacteria help balance the gut microbiota, which plays a key role in digestion, nutrient absorption, and immune function. By incorporating fermented pickles into your diet, you're not only enjoying a delicious and tangy snack but also promoting gut health and overall well-being.

Fermented foods are also more bioavailable than their non-fermented counterparts. The fermentation process breaks down certain compounds in vegetables that can inhibit nutrient absorption, making nutrients like iron, zinc, and B vitamins more accessible to the body. Additionally, fermented pickles are often rich in fiber, which supports digestive health and regular bowel movements.

When to Enjoy Fermented Pickles

Fermented pickles are a fantastic addition to many dishes, from salads and sandwiches to cheese platters and charcuterie boards. They also make an excellent snack on their own, providing a satisfying crunch and tang. Fermented pickles are perfect for adding complexity to a meal or as a flavorful side dish.

You can enjoy fermented pickles as soon as they are ready, but if you can wait, the flavors will continue to develop over time, giving you even more enjoyment with each bite. Store them in the fridge to preserve the probiotics and keep the pickles fresh for weeks to come.

Hot Pack Pickling: Long-Term Preservation

Hot pack pickling is a reliable method for preserving vegetables that provides an extended shelf life and a flavorful outcome. This technique involves packing your vegetables into sterilized jars and pouring a hot brine or pickling solution over them, followed by processing the jars in a boiling water bath. The heat from the brine and the subsequent canning process ensures that the pickles are sealed, creating an airtight environment that helps prevent spoilage while preserving the pickles for several months.

The Process of Hot Pack Pickling

Hot pack pickling begins by preparing your vegetables and making the brine or pickling solution. The vegetables are usually blanched or preheated in boiling water to soften them and to prepare them to absorb the brine. For example, cucumbers, beans, or carrots may be briefly cooked to help them absorb the pickling liquid more efficiently. Once the vegetables are ready, the hot brine typically made from vinegar, water, salt, and sugar is poured over the vegetables, which are packed tightly into sterilized jars.

One of the key benefits of this method is that the vegetables are heated, which helps to kill any bacteria or microorganisms that might cause spoilage, ensuring a safe and long-lasting product. The brine, made of vinegar or other acidic solutions, provides the tangy flavor we associate with pickles. This method also helps in sealing the jars properly, creating a vacuum that extends the shelf life of the pickles, which can last for several months when stored in a cool, dark place.

After the jars are filled with the vegetables and brine, they are processed by placing them in a boiling water bath. The processing time varies based on the size of the jars and the type of vegetable being pickled, but generally, it lasts anywhere from 5 to 20 minutes. This step not only ensures that the jars are sealed tightly, but it also sterilizes the contents, which is essential for preventing contamination.

Advantages of Hot Pack Pickling

One of the primary advantages of hot pack pickling is its ability to preserve food for an extended period of time. Unlike refrigerator pickles or quick pickles, which require refrigeration and have a limited shelf life, hot pack pickles are sealed in jars that can be stored at room temperature. When done properly, hot pack pickles can last for up to a year or more, making them ideal for long-term food storage.

This method also provides a consistent and uniform result. The vegetables in hot pack pickles are fully immersed in the brine, ensuring that they are evenly flavored. The heat from the brine allows the flavors to penetrate deeply into the vegetables, resulting in a more developed and tangy taste. Additionally, the vegetables tend to retain their shape and texture during the pickling process, making them perfect for preserving their crispness while still achieving that satisfying sourness.

When to Use Hot Pack Pickling

Hot pack pickling is ideal for vegetables that you want to store for the long term. Cucumbers, carrots, beans, cauliflower, and peppers are some of the most common vegetables that are preserved using this method. Hot pack pickling is also suitable for large batches, which makes it an excellent choice for seasonal harvests or for preserving produce from a local farmer's market.

The beauty of hot pack pickling is that it works for both standard and exotic vegetables, and it can be used for both sweet and sour pickles. By adjusting the spices and the ratio of vinegar to sugar, you can create a wide variety of pickled products, from spicy hot peppers to sweet, tangy bread-and-butter pickles.

Tips for Successful Hot Pack Pickling

To get the best results with hot pack pickling, it's important to use fresh, high-quality vegetables. Overripe vegetables may become mushy during the pickling process, so always choose firm, crisp vegetables. It's also important to sterilize the jars and lids properly to prevent contamination. Make sure the brine is boiling hot when poured over the vegetables to ensure proper sealing.

Another important tip is to leave the correct amount of headspace in the jars. This is the gap between the top of the brine and the rim of the jar. If you fill the jars too full, the brine may spill over during the canning process, compromising the seal. On the other hand, if you leave too much space, the pickles may not be properly preserved. Typically, a 1/4-inch headspace is ideal for most hot pack pickles.

Lastly, be mindful of the processing time. If the jars are not processed long enough, they may not seal properly, leading to spoilage. On the other hand, over-processing can make the pickles soft or mushy. Always follow the recommended processing times in your recipe, adjusting based on your altitude or the type of vegetable you are pickling.

Cold Pack Pickling: Fresh, Crisp, and Simple

Cold pack pickling is one of the simplest and most straightforward methods of preserving vegetables. Unlike hot pack pickling, which involves heating the vegetables and brine before sealing, cold pack pickling requires no heat and is perfect for those who want to preserve the fresh, crisp texture of their vegetables. This method is typically used for quick pickles or refrigerator pickles, where the vegetables are packed raw into jars and then covered with a brine solution.

The Process of Cold Pack Pickling

The process of cold pack pickling starts with selecting fresh, firm vegetables. The beauty of cold pack pickling lies in its simplicity; the vegetables are not pre-cooked or blanched, so they retain their natural crunch. This method works best with vegetables that have a firm texture, such as cucumbers, carrots, or green beans, and can also be used for fruits like peaches or pears if you want to try something a bit different.

Once you've selected your vegetables, it's time to pack them into sterilized jars. You can either slice or leave them whole depending on your preference. The next step is preparing your brine, which typically consists of water, vinegar, salt, and sometimes sugar. The brine may be flavored with spices such as mustard seeds, dill, coriander, or garlic, depending on the type of pickle you're making. Once the brine is ready, simply pour it over the vegetables in the jar, leaving enough headspace at the top to allow for expansion and avoid spillage.

After sealing the jar, the pickles are left to sit in a cool, dark place for several days to allow the brine to infuse the vegetables with flavor. The cooling process, rather than heating, helps to maintain the vegetables' crispness and fresh flavor, which is what makes cold pack pickling so appealing for those who want to preserve the "just picked" taste.

Advantages of Cold Pack Pickling

One of the primary advantages of cold pack pickling is the preservation of the vegetables' natural texture. Unlike hot pack pickling, where the vegetables soften due to the heat, cold pack pickling allows the produce to maintain a fresh crunch, making it ideal for those who prefer a crisp pickle. Additionally, the simplicity of this method makes it a great option for beginners or for anyone who wants to make pickles quickly without requiring a long preparation time.

Cold pack pickling also offers a more subtle flavor profile compared to hot pack pickles. The brine in cold pack pickling is usually less intense since the vegetables are not subjected to high heat. This means the brine flavors have a chance to slowly infuse into the vegetables, making cold pack pickles a great choice for more delicate or milder tasting vegetables. The result is a refreshing pickle that can serve as a snack or complement dishes without overwhelming them.

Another significant advantage of cold pack pickling is its versatility. You can make small batches of pickles in just a few hours and enjoy them within a few days. Cold pack pickles are typically stored in the refrigerator and can be eaten in a short amount of time, perfect for those who want a quick pickle without the need for long-term storage.

When to Use Cold Pack Pickling

Cold pack pickling is perfect for those who want to preserve fresh, in-season vegetables without compromising their crispness. This method works especially well with cucumbers, beans, carrots, and other vegetables that retain their firmness. Cold pack pickling is also a great way to pickle vegetables like radishes, cauliflower, and even fruits such as watermelon rind or pears, allowing for a variety of flavors and textures.

Additionally, cold pack pickling is ideal for small batch pickling. Whether you have a small garden or simply want to preserve a few vegetables, this method lets you pickle a variety of produce without needing to invest in large amounts of brine or equipment. It's perfect for those looking to experiment with flavors and textures without committing to a huge quantity.

Tips for Successful Cold Pack Pickling

To get the best results with cold pack pickling, start with fresh, high-quality vegetables. Overripe or soft vegetables may not retain their crispness, so it's important to use firm, fresh produce for the best outcome. If you're using cucumbers, make sure to select pickling cucumbers, which are specifically designed for pickling and have a firmer texture than regular cucumbers.

Using filtered or non-chlorinated water is important when making your brine. Chlorine can interfere with the pickling process and affect the flavor of the brine. If you only have access to tap water, letting it sit for a few hours will help the chlorine dissipate before use.

When preparing your brine, don't forget to taste it before pouring it over the vegetables. This is your opportunity to adjust the flavor balance, whether you want to add more sugar for sweetness, more vinegar for tang, or more spices for heat. Experimenting with the brine ensures that your pickles will turn out just the way you like them.

Lastly, remember that cold pack pickles usually require refrigeration and have a shorter shelf life than hot pack pickles. They are perfect for quick pickling but may not last as long as other pickling methods. Enjoy them within a few weeks for the best taste and texture.

Pickling for Preservation

Pickling is one of the most effective methods for preserving the flavors of seasonal produce and extending the shelf life of fruits, vegetables, and even meats. While pickling enhances flavors, its primary purpose is to ensure food remains safe and edible for an extended period. This is particularly helpful when you have an abundance of fresh produce that would otherwise spoil before you can enjoy it. Pickling for preservation involves creating an environment that keeps harmful bacteria and mold at bay, while promoting the growth of beneficial bacteria that help preserve the food.

The process of pickling starts with creating the right brine mixture of water, vinegar, and salt that creates an acidic environment, which is inhospitable to harmful bacteria but perfect for the beneficial microbes needed for preservation. Vinegar-based pickling works by using acid to preserve the food, while fermentation-based pickling relies on natural bacteria to create the necessary acid over time. Both methods ensure that food can be stored and enjoyed long after its harvest.

In addition to its role in preventing spoilage, the salt in pickling helps extract moisture from the vegetables, which creates a brine that allows the preservation process to begin. Sugar is often included in the brine to balance the acidity and enhance the flavor, but its role in preservation is secondary to salt and vinegar. For vegetables that need a higher level of acidity for safety, such as tomatoes or asparagus, it's important to use high-acid vinegar, such as distilled white vinegar or apple cider vinegar.

For long-term preservation, the pickled vegetables are typically processed using a method like water bath canning or pressure canning. The jars of pickles are sealed and processed in boiling water to kill any remaining bacteria or yeast, while also creating a vacuum seal. This vacuum seal is crucial in preventing contamination and ensuring that the food remains preserved for months, even years, without refrigeration.

When it comes to storing your pickled foods, the storage conditions are just as important as the pickling process itself. Pickles should be stored in a cool, dark place (ideally between 50-70°F), such as a pantry, cellar, or cupboard. Proper storage ensures that the pickles maintain their flavor, texture, and nutritional value. It's also important to check the jars periodically to ensure the seals are intact and that the pickles haven't been compromised.

In addition to traditional vegetable pickles, pickling can also be used for preserving fruits like peaches, pears, and even watermelon rinds. These pickled fruits provide a delightful, tangy complement to meals and can be used in both savory and sweet dishes. The pickling method for fruits may differ slightly, as they often require sweeter brines, but the preservation principle remains the same.

By mastering the art of pickling for preservation, you not only extend the shelf life of your harvest, but also enjoy the fruits of your labor throughout the year. The pickling process opens up a world of possibilities for enjoying seasonal produce at its peak, no matter what time of year it is.

Classic Pickle Recipes

Classic Dill Pickles: Perfectly Tangy and Crisp

One of the most beloved pickle varieties, classic dill pickles are tangy, crisp, and absolutely addictive. These pickles capture the essence of summer, and with the right technique, you can make them in your own kitchen.

To make dill pickles, start by selecting fresh cucumbers. Look for firm, unwaxed cucumbers that are about 4–6 inches long. Smaller cucumbers tend to be crisper and have fewer seeds, which is perfect for pickling.Fresh, high-quality cucumbers will yield the best results, so if you're picking them from your garden or the farmer's market, make sure they're as fresh as possible.

Ingredients:

- 4 pounds small cucumbers, firm and unwaxed
- 16 cloves garlic, peeled and blanched
- 8 fresh sprigs of dill
- 24 black peppercorns (3 peppercorns per jar)
- 2 quarts white vinegar
- 1/2 cup pickling salt

Instructions:

Start by soaking the cucumbers in a large bowl of ice water overnight to help them stay crisp. The next day, rinse and dry the cucumbers, then sterilize 8 pint-sized mason jars by boiling them for 10 minutes. Once the jars are prepared, pack the cucumbers tightly, adding 2 peeled garlic cloves, 1 sprig of dill, and 3 black peppercorns to each jar. In a large pot, bring 2 quarts of water to a boil, then add the vinegar and pickling salt, boiling for 5 minutes to dissolve the salt completely.

Carefully pour the hot brine over the cucumbers in the jars, leaving 1/4-inch of headspace at the top. Wipe the rims of the jars, seal them, and process the jars in a boiling water bath for 10 minutes, starting when the water reaches a full boil. After processing, remove the jars, let them cool to room temperature, and store them in a cool, dark place for at least 24–48 hours before opening. For the best flavor, allow the pickles to sit for 2 weeks before enjoying.

Pickled Onions: Sweet and Sour Perfection

Pickled onions offer a delicious sweet and tangy bite, perfect for adding a burst of flavor to salads, sandwiches, or even grilled meats. With their subtle spice from cloves and mace, they develop an irresistible depth of flavor over time. Let these pickled onions rest for at least 2 weeks before enjoying them to allow the flavors to fully marinate.

Ingredients:

- 1 red onion, thinly sliced (a mandoline works best for even slices)
- 1/2 cup apple cider vinegar
- 1 tablespoon granulated sugar
- 1 1/2 teaspoons salt
- 1 cup hot water (not boiling)

Instructions:

Begin by slicing the red onion as thinly as possible. If you have a mandoline, it will ensure uniform slices, but a sharp knife works just fine too. Pack the sliced onions tightly into a clean jar or bowl (a jar is easier for storing in the fridge).

In a measuring cup, combine the apple cider vinegar, sugar, salt, and warm water. Stir well until the sugar and salt have fully dissolved into the liquid. Pour the pickling mixture over the onions, ensuring they are fully submerged in the brine. Let the mixture sit at room temperature for an hour to allow the flavors to meld.

Once the onions have marinated, cover the jar or bowl and place them in the refrigerator. These quick pickled onions will be ready to enjoy after an hour, but for best results, let them sit for at least a few hours or up to 3 weeks in the fridge. The flavors will intensify and develop more complexity the longer they sit.

Pickled Beets: Vibrant and Flavorful

Pickled beets are a beautiful and flavorful way to preserve this earthy root vegetable. Their deep, rich color and tangy-sweet brine make them a perfect addition to salads, sandwiches, or enjoyed on their own. With their natural sweetness and slight acidity, pickled beets offer a delightful balance of flavors that brighten up any meal.

Ingredients:

- 4 medium beets
- 2 cups white vinegar
- 2 cups sugar
- 1 whole clove
- 1 cinnamon stick (1-inch)

Instructions:

Start by cooking the beets until they're tender, about 30 minutes, then remove the skins and slice them lengthwise into desired thickness. In a separate pan, combine the vinegar, sugar, clove, and cinnamon stick, and bring the mixture to a boil. Stir until the sugar dissolves completely, then remove from heat.

Pack the sliced beets into sterilized mason jars or a heatproof bowl, then pour the hot brine over the beets, ensuring they are completely covered. Let the beets cool to room temperature, then refrigerate them. Allow the pickled beets to sit for at least 3 days before enjoying them, though they'll continue to develop flavor over time. Keep the pickled beets refrigerated for long-lasting flavor.

Pickled Carrots: Crunchy and Spicy

Pickled carrots are a fantastic snack on their own or a crunchy addition to salads and wraps. With a hint of spice from the garlic and peppercorns, they offer a delightful flavor that will leave you craving more.

Ingredients:

- 4 to 6 carrots, peeled and sliced
- 1 cup white vinegar
- 1/2 cup sugar
- 1/2 tablespoon mixed pickling spice

Instructions:

Start by packing the peeled and sliced carrots into a pint-sized mason jar, ensuring they fit snugly but with a little room left at the top. In a separate glass or enamel saucepan, combine the white vinegar, sugar, pickling spice, and 1/4 cup of water. Bring the mixture to a boil, then let it simmer for 10 minutes to allow the flavors to meld together.

Once the brine is ready, carefully pour the hot liquid over the carrots in the jar, leaving about 1/4-inch of headspace at the top. Wipe the rim of the jar clean, seal it, and process the jar in a boiling water bath for 10 minutes, starting the timer once the water reaches a full boil. After processing, remove the jar, let it cool, and refrigerate. These carrot pickles are best enjoyed after sitting for at least 48 hours, but they'll continue to develop flavor the longer they rest.

Pickled Garlic: A Unique Twist for Any Meal

Pickled garlic may sound unusual, but it's an excellent way to enjoy the benefits of garlic while tempering its sharpness. The garlic cloves become milder, more aromatic, and the brine infuses them with flavor, making them a great addition to many dishes.

Ingredients:

- 10-12 cloves of garlic, peeled
- 1 cup white vinegar
- 1 cup water
- 1 tablespoon sugar
- 1 tablespoon kosher salt
- 2 sprigs of fresh thyme
- 1 teaspoon black peppercorns

Instructions:

Peel the garlic cloves, ensuring the skins are completely removed. In a saucepan, combine the vinegar, water, sugar, salt, thyme, and peppercorns. Bring the mixture to a boil, stirring to dissolve the sugar and salt.

Once the brine is ready, pack the peeled garlic cloves into a sterilized jar. Carefully pour the hot brine over the garlic, leaving about 1/4-inch of headspace. Seal the jar, allow it to cool to room temperature, and refrigerate. After a couple of days, the garlic will begin to develop its flavor, and it will continue to improve over time. These pickled garlic cloves will last for several weeks when stored properly in the fridge.

Pickled Mixed Vegetables: A Tangy, Colorful Medley

Pickled Mixed Vegetables offer a vibrant and flavorful twist on traditional pickles. This recipe allows you to pickle a variety of vegetables, combining them with a zesty brine infused with mustard and celery seeds. The crunch of fresh vegetables, combined with the tangy, slightly sweet brine, makes these pickles a perfect addition to any meal or as a snack.

Ingredients:

- 4 lbs 4- to 5-inch pickling cucumbers, washed and cut into 1-inch slices (cut off 1/16-inch from the blossom end and discard)
- 2 lbs peeled and quartered small onions
- 4 cups cut celery (1-inch pieces)
- 2 cups peeled and cut carrots (1/2-inch pieces)
- 2 cups cut sweet red peppers (1/2-inch pieces)
- 2 cups cauliflower flowerets
- 5 cups white vinegar (5%)

- 1/4 cup prepared mustard
- 1/2 cup canning or pickling salt
- 3-1/2 cups sugar
- 3 tbsp celery seed
- 2 tbsp mustard seed
- 1/2 tsp whole cloves
- 1/2 tsp ground turmeric

Instructions:

Begin by combining the vegetables in a large bowl, then cover with 2 inches of cubed or crushed ice. Refrigerate for 3–4 hours to allow the vegetables to chill. In an 8-quart kettle, mix the vinegar and mustard together. Add salt, sugar, celery seed, mustard seed, cloves, and turmeric, then bring the mixture to a boil.

Once the brine has boiled, drain the vegetables and add them to the hot pickling solution. Cover and bring the mixture back to a boil. After a few minutes, drain the vegetables, but reserve the brine. Pack the vegetables into hot, sterilized jars, leaving 1/2-inch of headspace. Pour the hot pickling solution over the vegetables, again leaving 1/2-inch of headspace. Wipe the rims of the jars, adjust the lids, and process in a boiling-water canner for 10 minutes.

Pickled Dilled Okra: A Crunchy, Spicy Snack

Pickled Dilled Okra offers a delightful, crunchy snack with the perfect balance of dill and heat. The tangy brine, paired with the fresh okra pods, creates a pickle that's perfect for serving as an appetizer, in salads, or enjoyed on its own.

Ingredients:

- 7 lbs small okra pods
- 6 small hot peppers (optional for extra spice)
- 4 tsp dill seed
- 8–9 garlic cloves
- 2/3 cup canning or pickling salt
- 6 cups water
- 6 cups vinegar (5%)

Instructions:

Start by washing and trimming the okra. Pack the hot jars tightly with whole okra, leaving 1/2-inch of headspace. Place one garlic clove in each jar. In a large saucepan, combine the salt, hot peppers (if using), dill seed, water, and vinegar, then bring to a boil. Pour the hot brine over the okra, leaving 1/2-inch of headspace. Remove air bubbles, adjust headspace if needed, wipe the rims of the jars with a clean, damp paper towel, and seal the jars. Process in a boiling-water canner for 10 minutes to ensure the pickles are properly preserved.

Dilly Beans: A Zesty, Herb-Infused Delight

Dilly Beans are a classic favorite, combining the crispness of green beans with the refreshing flavor of dill. These pickled beans are perfect for snacking, adding to salads, or as a tangy side dish. With a bit of cayenne pepper, they also offer a hint of heat, making them a favorite for spice lovers.

Ingredients:

- 2 lbs whole green beans, trimmed
- 1 tsp cayenne pepper
- 4 cloves garlic, blanched
- 4 heads dill
- 2-1/2 cups white vinegar
- 1/4 cup pickling salt

Instructions:

Pack the beans lengthwise into sterilized jars, leaving 1/4-inch of headspace. To each jar, add 1/4 teaspoon cayenne, 1 garlic clove, and 1 head of dill. In a saucepan, bring the vinegar and salt to a boil, then pour the hot liquid over the beans in the jars, leaving 1/2-inch of headspace. Seal the jars and process them in a boiling-water canner for 5 minutes, starting when the water begins to boil.

Pickled Radishes: A Bold and Crisp Snack

Pickled radishes are an easy and quick way to enjoy the spicy, crunchy texture of radishes with a tangy twist. These pickles are vibrant in color and flavor, offering a zesty kick that works well as an accompaniment to tacos, salads, or as a snack on their own.

Ingredients:

- 1 bunch radishes
- ¾ cup white wine vinegar or apple cider vinegar
- ¾ cup water
- 3 tablespoons honey or maple syrup
- 2 teaspoons salt
- 1 teaspoon red pepper flakes (for very spicy pickles; use ½ teaspoon for medium spicy or omit for milder pickles)
- ½ teaspoon whole mustard seeds (optional)
- Optional add-ins: garlic cloves, black peppercorns, fennel seeds, coriander seeds

Instructions:

Slice off the tops and bottoms of the radishes, then use a sharp knife or mandoline to slice them into thin rounds. Pack the radish slices into a pint-sized canning jar and top with red pepper flakes and mustard seeds (if using). In a saucepan, combine the vinegar, water, honey or maple syrup, and salt. Bring to a boil, stirring occasionally, then pour the brine over the radishes, ensuring they are fully covered. Let the mixture cool to room temperature before sealing the jar.

You can serve these pickles immediately or store them in the refrigerator for later. These radishes will stay fresh for up to 5 days, but their crispness and flavor are best enjoyed within the first few days after pickling.

Pickled Condiments and Relishes

In addition to traditional pickles, relishes provide a unique and flavorful twist to the pickling process, offering a versatile way to preserve fruits and vegetables. Relishes are essentially pickled foods that have been chopped or minced, often combined with tangy vinegars, sweeteners, and spices to create a chunky, zesty texture. This makes them an ideal accompaniment for a variety of dishes whether you're adding them to sandwiches, enjoying them as a snack, or topping your favorite grilled meats. Their bold flavors and vibrant colors bring a delightful contrast to savory dishes.

The beauty of relishes lies in their flexibility. Unlike traditional pickles, which maintain their whole shape and crispness, relishes are typically simmered, softening their texture and allowing the flavors to meld together. This allows the relish to be both tangy and savory, and they can be made from a wide array of vegetables and fruits, such as cucumbers, carrots, tomatoes, and cauliflower. In fact, you can even experiment with more unusual ingredients like watermelon rind or peaches to create exciting variations. While some relishes are sweet, others lean towards the spicy or tangy side, offering a balance to heavier, richer meals.

The pickling process for relishes is similar to traditional pickling, with the key difference being that the vegetables or fruits are chopped or minced before being pickled. The brine or vinegar solution is often infused with spices such as mustard seeds, garlic, turmeric, and cinnamon, adding depth and complexity to the final product. Once the relish has simmered to the desired consistency, it is packed into sterilized jars for long-term storage.

Making relish allows you to adjust the sweetness, heat, and tang to your personal taste. If you prefer a richer flavor, you can add brown sugar, mustard, or honey. For a spicier relish, ingredients like jalapeños, onion powder, and garlic can introduce the perfect amount of heat. The ability to customize your relish makes it an enjoyable and rewarding condiment to create, and one that will elevate any meal. The key is to experiment with different flavor combinations and find what works best for you.

Relishes are great for using up surplus produce, making them ideal for those looking to preserve the bounty of their garden or local farmer's market. Whether you make a spicy, sweet, or herb-infused relish, this pickling variation will allow you to enjoy bold, tangy flavors that bring new life to any dish.

Corn Relish

Corn relish is a sweet and tangy condiment, perfect for serving with meats, grilled vegetables, or as an accompaniment to summer barbecues. The combination of fresh corn, colorful peppers, onions, and cabbage creates a flavorful relish that will add a touch of sweetness to any dish. The acidity of the vinegar and the warmth of the spices make this relish a delightful addition to any meal.

Ingredients:

- 1 dozen ears of sweet corn
- 2 onions, chopped
- 2 green bell peppers, seeded and chopped
- 1 red bell pepper, seeded and chopped
- 1 cup chopped cabbage
- 2 cups white vinegar

- 1 cup sugar
- 2 tablespoons pickling salt
- 1-1/2 tablespoons ground mustard
- 1/4 teaspoon freshly ground black pepper

Instructions:

Start by cutting the corn from the cobs, but do not scrape the ears. In a large pot, combine the corn, onions, peppers, and cabbage. Add the vinegar, sugar, salt, mustard, and pepper, and cook slowly for about 1 hour, stirring often to avoid burning. Once the vegetables have softened and the mixture has thickened, pour the relish into sterilized jars, leaving 1/4-inch of headspace. Seal the jars and process them for 10 minutes in a boiling-water canner, starting when the water begins to boil. This recipe makes about 5 half-pint jars.

Hot Dog Relish

Hot Dog Relish is a classic, tangy, and slightly sweet condiment that works perfectly with hot dogs, hamburgers, or even as a topping for grilled meats. Its unique blend of green tomatoes, peppers, and spices will bring out a rich and zesty flavor in whatever dish it accompanies. The pickling process adds a delightful crunch, making it a must-have condiment for summer meals.

Ingredients:

- 6 green tomatoes
- 6 green bell peppers, seeded
- 2 onions, peeled
- 1/2 head cabbage, cored
- 1/4 cup pickling salt

- 3 cups white vinegar
- 3 cups sugar
- 1 tablespoon mustard seed
- 1 tablespoon celery seed
- 1 teaspoon turmeric
- 3 red bell peppers, seeded and finely chopped

Instructions:

In a food processor or grinder, shred the tomatoes, green bell peppers, onions, and cabbage. Sprinkle the salt over the shredded vegetables and let them stand overnight. After draining and rinsing the vegetables, bring the vinegar, sugar, mustard seed, celery seed, turmeric, and 1 cup of water to a boil for about 5 minutes. Add the tomato mixture and red bell peppers to the brine and simmer for an additional 10 minutes. Pour the hot relish into sterilized jars, leaving 1/4-inch of headspace. Seal the jars and process for 10 minutes in a boiling-water canner. This recipe makes about 5 pints.

Sweet Onion Relish

Sweet onion relish is a flavorful, tangy condiment that can enhance the taste of many dishes. The sweetness of the onions combined with the aromatic caraway seeds and tangy vinegar makes it a versatile topping. This relish pairs beautifully with grilled meats, cheeses, and even as a topping for crackers or toasted bread.

Ingredients:

- 2 cups chopped sweet onions
- 1/2 green bell pepper, seeded and diced
- 3 tablespoons diced pimiento
- 1/2 cup white vinegar
- 1/4 cup sugar

- 2 teaspoons caraway seed
- 1/2 teaspoon pickling salt

Instructions:

Combine the chopped onions, bell pepper, and pimiento in a bowl and set them aside. In a saucepan, bring the vinegar, sugar, caraway seeds, and pickling salt to a boil, then simmer for 5 minutes. Pour the hot brine over the onion mixture and refrigerate for several hours to allow the flavors to meld together. This recipe yields about 2-1/2 cups of relish.

Chapter 4
Advancing Your Pickling Skills

Understanding Different Pickling Methods

Pickling can be as simple or as complex as you want it to be. There are a variety of methods to explore, each with its own distinct characteristics. The method you choose can dramatically affect the flavor and texture of your pickles.

Quick Pickling: Fast and Easy Pickles

Quick pickling is one of the most beginner-friendly methods of pickling. As the name suggests, it's perfect for when you're in a hurry or simply want to make pickles without waiting for days or weeks. Quick pickles are made by soaking vegetables in a vinegar-based brine, often with the addition of salt, sugar, and spices. The vegetables absorb the brine's tangy flavor quickly, and within a few hours to a couple of days, your pickles are ready to eat.

Unlike fermented pickles, quick pickles do not require fermentation. This means you get a sharp, tangy pickle without the probiotic benefits that come from bacterial growth. Quick pickling is ideal for vegetables like cucumbers, carrots, onions, and peppers. The result is a crispy, tangy pickle with a satisfying crunch and flavor that can be customized with various herbs and spices.

Quick pickling is a versatile method, allowing you to experiment with flavors and vegetables. You can adjust the sweetness by adding more sugar, or increase the tanginess by using more vinegar. For a little heat, add chili flakes or mustard seeds. This method is particularly well-suited for beginners or those looking to preserve seasonal vegetables in a short amount of time.

Fermented Pickles: The Slow and Tangy Method

Fermented pickles are a more traditional approach, requiring patience and a bit more attention than quick pickling, but the results are well worth the wait. This process relies on the natural fermentation of vegetables through the activity of beneficial bacteria. When vegetables are submerged in a brine of water and salt, bacteria naturally present on the vegetables begin to feed on the sugars, producing lactic acid as a byproduct. This lactic acid preserves the vegetables and gives them their signature sour flavor.

The key difference between fermented and quick pickles is that fermented pickles do not use vinegar for preservation. Instead, the lactic acid bacteria create a tangy flavor over time. The result is a more complex, slightly sour pickle with a softer texture than quick pickles. The fermentation process takes longer, typically anywhere from a few days to several weeks, depending on the vegetable and the ambient temperature. It's a process that rewards patience, as the flavors deepen and develop over time.

Fermented pickles are also rich in probiotics, which are beneficial for gut health. The probiotics that grow during fermentation can help support digestion and boost your immune system. This makes fermented pickles a great option for those looking to add more probiotic-rich foods to their diet. Popular vegetables for fermentation include cucumbers (for classic dill pickles), carrots, beets, and cabbage (for sauerkraut).

Pickling for Different Flavors

Pickling allows for the creation of an endless variety of flavors, all depending on the combination of spices, herbs, and liquids used in the brine. Pickling for different flavors is where the art of pickling truly shinesit's an opportunity for creativity, experimentation, and custom tastes.

The brine used in pickling serves as the base for flavoring your vegetables or fruits. The most common brines include vinegar-based (using white, apple cider, or rice vinegar) or saltwater-based (used in fermentation). However, the flavor of the brine is not limited to vinegar and salt; it is enhanced by the choice of spices, herbs, and other flavoring agents.

Vinegar-based pickles, for instance, can be altered by adding spices like mustard seeds, dill, garlic, cinnamon, or cloves. These spices will infuse the brine, and in turn, the vegetables, with a unique, complex flavor. For sweet pickles, you might add sugar or honey to the brine, creating a tangy-sweet balance perfect for cucumbers, peppers, and even fruits. For spicy pickles, adding chili flakes, jalapeños, or whole peppercorns can infuse the brine with a sharp heat that enhances the flavor profile.

Fermented pickles, on the other hand, have a more subtle flavor profile that develops as the vegetables ferment over time. As lactic acid bacteria consume the sugars in the vegetables, they produce lactic acid, which gives these pickles their signature tangy taste. Fermentation creates a depth of flavor that is typically less sharp than vinegar-based pickles, with a slight sourness that comes from the fermentation process. You can still enhance fermented pickles by adding herbs such as rosemary, thyme, bay leaves, and oregano, which will all contribute to the natural flavors of the fermentation.

Experimenting with different herbs and spices will help create pickles that are uniquely yours. For example, ginger, cinnamon sticks, and cloves can add warmth and sweetness to your brine, perfect for pickled apples, pears, or carrots. If you prefer an Asian-inspired flavor, you can try adding ginger, garlic, star anise, and soy sauce to your brine for a more umami-filled pickle, perfect for radishes or cucumbers.

In addition, for fruit pickles, consider pairing fruits like peaches, apples, or mangoes with a spicy or sweet brine that combines cinnamon, nutmeg, and cloves with sugar and vinegar. These sweet-and-tangy combinations work especially well with summer fruits, which can be preserved and enjoyed throughout the year.

Pickling for Different Textures

While flavor is often the primary consideration in pickling, texture is just as important. The texture of your pickles can make all the difference between a good pickle and a great one. Whether you prefer pickles that retain their crunch or ones that soften over time, you can control the texture of your pickled vegetables using a variety of techniques.

Quick pickling yields crisp, fresh textures, which is perfect for people who enjoy the satisfying crunch of vegetables like cucumbers, carrots, and green beans. The acid in the vinegar helps preserve the vegetables, while the salt draws moisture out, making them firm. This method is ideal when you're in a hurry, and the vegetables are not left to ferment long enough to soften. For a crunchier pickle, avoid overcooking the vegetables when heating them in the brine and store them at room temperature for a shorter time.

In contrast, fermented pickles develop a different texture over time. The natural bacteria in the brine break down the cell walls of the vegetables, resulting in a softer, more pliable texture. While some people prefer a softer texture, others like to maintain a bit of crunch, so controlling the fermentation time is crucial. If you're looking for a firm texture in your fermented pickles, you can store them at cooler temperatures to slow down the fermentation process and prevent over-softening.

The salt concentration also plays a key role in achieving the desired texture. A higher concentration of salt will keep vegetables firmer by drawing out more moisture, while a lower concentration may allow the vegetables to soften more quickly. You'll want to experiment with different salt-to-water ratios to achieve the texture you desire. Pickling weights and submerging lids are also important tools to help maintain a uniform texture throughout your pickles.

Another method to preserve texture is hot pack pickling, where vegetables are briefly heated in brine before being packed into jars. This technique ensures that the pickles retain a tender yet crisp texture even after being processed in the boiling water canner. Cold pack pickling, which involves packing raw vegetables into jars and covering them with hot brine, can help maintain the fresh crunch of the pickled vegetables, especially when using high-quality, fresh ingredients.

Finally, if you prefer a soft pickle for certain vegetables, like onions or beans, you can simply allow them to ferment longer or adjust the ratio of salt and brine to suit your texture preferences.

Pickled Jalapenos: A Spicy Kick for Your Pantry

Pickled jalapenos add a bold, spicy flavor to everything from tacos to sandwiches, offering the perfect balance of heat and tang. With their crisp texture and zesty brine, they're a must-have for any spice lover's pantry.

Ingredients:

- 1 cup vinegar (white or apple cider vinegar)
- 1 cup water
- 2 tablespoons white sugar
- 1 tablespoon salt
- 2 cloves garlic, smashed
- 1 pound jalapeño peppers, thinly sliced

Instructions:

Start by combining the vinegar, water, sugar, salt, and garlic in a pot over medium-high heat. Stir the mixture until the sugar and salt dissolve completely. Once the brine comes to a boil, remove the pot from the heat.

Stir the sliced jalapeños into the brine and let the mixture sit for about 15 minutes, allowing the peppers to slightly soften and absorb the flavors. Then, using tongs or a slotted spoon, transfer the jalapeños into a sterilized mason jar, packing them tightly.

Pour the hot brine over the jalapeños, making sure they're fully covered. Let the jar cool to room temperature for about 30 minutes. Once cooled, seal the jar and refrigerate. The pickled jalapeños will be ready to enjoy after 24 hours, but the flavors will continue to develop over time. They'll keep in the fridge for up to a month.

Pickled Cauliflower: Colorful and Flavorful

Pickled cauliflower offers a vibrant crunch that adds color and a tangy twist to any dish. Its firm texture holds up well in the brine, making it an ideal candidate for pickling.

Ingredients:

- 3 cups cauliflower florets (purple or white)
- 1 small white or red onion, thinly sliced
- 5 dried arbol chiles, torn up
- 2 teaspoons black mustard seeds
- 1 1/2 cups rice vinegar
- 1 cup water
- 1 tablespoon fine grain sea salt
- 3 tablespoons sugar

Instructions:

Start by tossing the cauliflower florets, onion slices, arbol chiles, and mustard seeds in a medium bowl. Once well mixed, transfer the mixture to a clean quart-sized mason jar, packing the ingredients tightly so they fill nearly to the top.

In a saucepan over medium heat, combine the rice vinegar, water, salt, and sugar. Bring the mixture to a simmer, stirring occasionally until the sugar dissolves. Once the brine is ready, carefully pour it into the mason jar, covering the cauliflower mixture. Leave about 1/2-inch of space at the top of the jar.

Seal the jar tightly, let it cool to room temperature, and then refrigerate. The pickled cauliflower will be ready to enjoy within a day, though the flavors will continue to develop over time. For the best results, use within a week.

Pressure Canning for Pickles

Pressure canning is an essential skill for anyone interested in pickling as a method of long-term preservation. While water bath canning is great for high-acid foods like fruits and some vegetables, pressure canning is required for low-acid foods, which are more prone to spoilage. Pickling through pressure canning ensures that your vegetables stay preserved and safe for consumption over long periods, even without refrigeration.

The pressure canning process is designed to increase the temperature inside the canning jar, which kills harmful bacteria, yeasts, and molds that could lead to spoilage. This method is especially important when pickling low-acid vegetables like green beans, asparagus, or carrots, which cannot be safely preserved using just vinegar and a water bath. Pressure canning raises the temperature of the food inside the jar to above the boiling point of water, typically around 240°F to 250°F. This high temperature destroys any bacteria, including Clostridium botulinum, the bacteria responsible for botulism, a rare but serious form of food poisoning.

The process begins by preparing your pickles as you normally would by making your brine, slicing your vegetables, and packing them into sterilized jars. The only difference with pressure canning is that, after the jars are filled, they must be processed in a pressure canner rather than a simple boiling water bath. The pressure canner is a specialized pot that has a locking lid and a pressure gauge, which allows you to build and maintain the required pressure for safe canning.

The key to successful pressure canning is to follow the recommended processing times for the specific type of pickle you are preserving. For example, green beans might need to be processed for 25-30 minutes at 10-15 pounds of pressure depending on your altitude, while pickled asparagus may require a slightly longer time. These times are designed to ensure that the vegetables reach the necessary temperature to kill harmful bacteria, and they vary based on the size of the jars and the type of vegetable.

Once the jars are processed, they need to be sealed and cooled. After cooling, you should check that the lids have sealed properly (there should be no popping sound when pressed). If the lid pops back up, the jar has not sealed properly and should be refrigerated or reprocessed. Store the sealed jars in a cool, dark place for long-term preservation. Pickles made with pressure canning can last for up to a year, and sometimes even longer, without spoiling.

One important thing to note when pressure canning is to always use specific canning recipes and ensure you're using the correct measurements of ingredients, especially vinegar, salt, and sugar, as this guarantees the acidity level is sufficient for safe preservation. Don't adjust the recipe proportions unless you're experienced with canning, as small variations can impact the safety of the preserved food.

Advantages of Pressure Canning for Pickles:

1. **Increased Shelf Life**: Pressure canning provides a much longer shelf life compared to other preservation methods like refrigerator pickling or water-bath canning.
2. **Safety**: The high temperature kills dangerous bacteria, ensuring that your pickles are safe to eat long after their shelf life would expire under other methods.
3. **Versatility**: It allows you to pickle low-acid vegetables that cannot be safely pickled using vinegar alone, such as beans, carrots, and cauliflower.

Disadvantages of Pressure Canning:

1. **Specialized Equipment**: A pressure canner is an investment that requires regular maintenance to ensure safe use.
2. **Longer Processing Times**: The pressure canning process takes longer than water-bath canning, which may require patience and more attention to detail.
3. **Takes Practice**: It's important to follow recipes and times exactly to avoid underprocessing or overprocessing, which could compromise the pickles' flavor or safety.

How to Troubleshoot Common Pickling Problems

While pickling can be an enjoyable and relatively simple process, there are a few challenges that may arise during your pickling adventures. It's important to know how to troubleshoot these common problems so that you can ensure your pickles turn out just right. Below are some common issues you may encounter, along with tips for fixing them and preventing them in the future.

Cloudy Brine

A cloudy brine can often be a sign that something went wrong during the pickling process. Typically, the most common culprit is the use of iodized salt instead of pickling salt. Iodized salt contains additives, such as iodine, which can cause the brine to turn cloudy and affect the clarity of your pickles. To avoid this problem, always opt for pickling salt or kosher salt when pickling. These salts do not contain any additives that could cloud your brine or alter the texture of your vegetables.

Another possible reason for cloudy brine is insufficiently dissolved salt in the brine mixture. It's important to fully dissolve the salt in the brine by stirring it properly before pouring it over your vegetables. If the brine was not brought to a full boil, the salt might not have dissolved properly, leading to a cloudy or uneven brine. Make sure to dissolve the salt completely by heating it in the brine solution before using it for pickling. By following these steps, you can ensure your brine remains clear and your pickles maintain their visual appeal.

Mushy Pickles

Soft, mushy pickles are a common disappointment for picklers, and they can occur for several reasons. One of the main causes of this issue is using overripe cucumbers or cucumbers that were not fresh enough when they were pickled. Cucumbers that have already begun to soften or ripen will lose their firmness when pickled, resulting in a mushy texture. To prevent this, always use fresh, firm cucumbers that are still in their prime. Avoid cucumbers that are too soft or have wrinkles, as they will not retain their desired crispness.

Another factor contributing to mushy pickles could be the soaking time before pickling. Cucumbers should ideally be soaked in ice water for several hours prior to pickling, as this helps to firm up their texture and ensures they remain crisp during the pickling process. If you skipped this step or didn't soak the cucumbers for long enough, you may find that your pickles turn out soft. Make sure to soak the cucumbers in cold water for several hours, preferably overnight, before beginning the pickling process.

Flavor Imbalance

One of the most important aspects of pickling is achieving the right balance of flavors, particularly between the salty and sweet components of the brine. If your pickles taste too salty, it's likely that the salt-to-water ratio was off or that you used too much salt in the brine. If your brine tastes too sweet, you may have added too much sugar. Adjusting the vinegar-to-sugar ratio can help you find the perfect balance of acidity and sweetness for your pickles.

Before pouring the brine over your vegetables, it's essential to taste the brine to make sure it has the right flavor. You can always tweak the brine by adding a bit more sugar if it's too sour or more vinegar if it's too sweet. Keep in mind that the flavors will intensify as the pickles sit and marinate, so it's better to start with a slightly milder brine and adjust accordingly. Don't hesitate to experiment with different vinegar varieties (such as apple cider vinegar or white vinegar) to find the flavor profile that works best for your pickles.

Fermentation Failures

Fermented pickles, such as those made with the lacto-fermentation method, require special care during the fermentation process. One of the most crucial factors in fermentation is ensuring that the vegetables are fully submerged in the brine. If the vegetables are not fully covered, they will be exposed to air, which can lead to spoilage, mold, or undesirable bacteria growth. To prevent this, use a fermentation weight or other methods to keep the vegetables submerged throughout the fermentation process. A clean, tight-fitting lid or makeshift weight can help keep your pickles under the brine, allowing the fermentation to proceed properly.

If you notice any mold growing on the surface of your fermented pickles, it's important to discard the batch immediately. Mold can be harmful and is a sign that the fermentation environment was not properly maintained. Mold growth usually occurs when there is too much exposure to air, which can happen if the vegetables are not submerged or the jar was not sealed correctly. Always monitor your pickles during the fermentation process, and if you encounter mold, do not attempt to salvage the batch. It's best to start fresh with properly submerged vegetables.

By understanding these common issues and following these troubleshooting tips, you can avoid the pitfalls that lead to poor results. With a little care and attention, your pickling and fermenting will result in delicious, crisp, and flavorful pickles every time. Don't be discouraged by a batch that didn't turn out perfectly. Use it as an opportunity to learn and improve for the next one!

Pickling Spice: Create Your Own Custom Spice Blends

A signature spice blend is one of the easiest ways to elevate your pickles and ferments. Pickling spice is a fragrant mix of herbs and spices that adds depth and complexity to the brine, enhancing the flavor of whatever you're pickling. The great thing about creating your own pickling spice is that you can tailor it to your personal tastes. Whether you prefer something more savory, sweet, or spicy, this recipe will help you craft the perfect blend to suit your needs.

This homemade pickling spice blend can be added to any pickle recipe, from classic cucumber pickles to more creative options like pickled beets, carrots, or even fruits. Plus, the aroma of freshly ground spices will make your kitchen smell irresistible.

Pickling Spice Blend

Ingredients:

- 1 dried hot red pepper (chili), broken into small pieces or crushed
- 1 small piece of dried ginger
- 2 bay leaves, crushed
- 2 cinnamon sticks, broken into small pieces
- 1 tablespoon whole black peppercorns
- 1 teaspoon cloves
- 1 teaspoon dill seeds
- 1 teaspoon coriander seeds
- 1 teaspoon crumbled whole mace
- 1 tablespoon whole allspice
- 1 teaspoon juniper berries
- 1 tablespoon mustard seeds
- Salt (to taste)

Directions:

Start by breaking the dried hot red chili into small pieces or crushing it. Then, pound the dried ginger and crush the bay leaves using a mortar and pestle. If you don't have a mortar and pestle, a grinder on low speed is acceptable, but avoid over-grinding to preserve the spices' aromatic qualities.

Next, break the cinnamon sticks into smaller pieces, and then combine all the remaining spices in a bowl. Mix the spices well to ensure an even blend. Once mixed, your pickling spice is ready to be added to your pickling recipes or homemade sauces.

Store the spice blend in an airtight container for future use. It will keep for several months, and the fragrance will only get better with time.

Tips and Variations:

To maintain the full aroma and preservation qualities of the spices, avoid using an electric grinder or mixer. Instead, use a mortar and pestle to crush the spices by hand, as this prevents the spices from overheating and losing their essence.

Adjust the heat: If you prefer a milder spice, reduce the number of hot chilies or replace them with a sweeter pepper. For extra heat, feel free to add more dried chili or a pinch of cayenne.

Sweetness: For sweeter pickles, you can add a bit more cinnamon or allspice to your blend.

Storage: Store the spice blend in a cool, dry place in an airtight container. For longer shelf life, consider sealing the jar with a vacuum lid to lock in freshness.

Serving Ideas:

Use your custom pickling spice in any of the following:

- Pickled Mango, Pickled Lime, or Pickled Carrots for a traditional sweet-tangy flavor.
- Pickled Red Chili for a spicy kick.
- Cucumber Pickles with a fresh and balanced tang.
- Pickled Beets, Pickled Zucchini, or Pickled Cauliflower for a crunchy, aromatic bite.
- Add to sauces or marinades to infuse flavor into your dishes.

Chapter 5
Getting Started with Fermentation

Fermentation is one of the oldest methods of preserving food, and it offers more than just preservation. The process creates foods rich in probiotics, which can support your digestive health and enhance the nutritional value of your meals. This chapter will introduce you to the basics of fermentation, starting with simple recipes like sauerkraut, a classic fermented dish, and an introduction to kimchi, a more complex fermentation that we'll explore in detail in the next chapter.

What is Fermentation?

Fermentation is a natural, age-old process that uses microorganisms, such as bacteria and yeast, to break down sugars in food. As these microorganisms consume sugars, they convert them into beneficial compounds like acids and alcohol, which preserve the food and enhance its flavor. In the case of vegetable fermentation, lactic acid bacteria (LAB) are the key players, turning sugars into lactic acid, which gives fermented foods their characteristic sourness and provides their preservation benefits.

Beyond just preserving food, fermentation enriches it with probiotics like microorganisms that are beneficial to our health. These probiotics, including Lactobacillus and Bifidobacterium, have a significant impact on gut health, supporting digestion, promoting a balanced gut microbiome, and boosting immune function. Foods such as sauerkraut, kimchi, yogurt, and kefir are all products of fermentation that contain these beneficial bacteria. Over centuries, fermentation has been used as a means of food preservation and health enhancement, offering a natural way to increase the nutritional value of foods and improve digestion without relying on artificial additives.

Fermented foods are also rich in enzymes, which help break down nutrients and improve digestion. Additionally, fermentation increases the bioavailability of certain nutrients, making them easier for your body to absorb. For instance, fermenting dairy can increase the availability of calcium, and fermented vegetables can boost the bioavailability of B vitamins and minerals. The ongoing research into fermentation and probiotics continues to reveal the many health benefits of these ancient practices, further solidifying their place in modern diets.

Temperature and Fermentation

One of the most critical factors in achieving a successful fermentation process is temperature. Temperature influences how fast or slow the fermentation process occurs and can also impact the flavor, texture, and safety of the final product. Generally, most fermentation processes work best in a temperature range between 60°F and 75°F (15°C–24°C), with room temperature being ideal for most vegetable and dairy ferments.

Too high a temperature can accelerate the fermentation process, leading to overly sour or overly acidic foods. When fermentation happens too quickly, the flavors may develop in an unbalanced way, leading to off flavors or even spoiling the food. Moreover, high temperatures (typically above 80°F or 27°C) can encourage the growth of undesirable bacteria and molds, which can compromise the safety of the food.

On the other hand, low temperatures (below 55°F or 13°C) can slow fermentation down significantly, potentially halting the process altogether. Fermentation becomes sluggish, and the beneficial bacteria may not thrive as they should. For dairy products such as yogurt and kefir, maintaining a warm, stable environment is critical for setting the texture and flavor. This is why yogurt makers or fermentation chambers are often used to create and maintain the perfect warm environment for these kinds of ferments.

To achieve the best results, it's important to control the temperature during fermentation. While fermenting vegetables like sauerkraut or kimchi, a cool room temperature (around 65°F–70°F) is often ideal. If you live in a warm climate and don't have a cool cellar or basement, consider using fermentation wraps, temperature-controlled fermentation crocks, or even fermentation chambers to maintain a steady, cool environment. These tools help regulate temperature, providing a stable environment for your cultures to flourish and ensuring consistent results.

For those of you who are experimenting with fermented beverages like kombucha or water kefir, the same principle applies: they also require a controlled environment. During warmer months, you may find that your fermenting jars or bottles heat up too much, leading to over-fermentation. In that case, it's important to monitor the temperature, keeping the environment around 70°F–75°F (21°C–24°C) for optimal results.

How to Maintain Optimal Fermentation Conditions

Fermentation thrives when conditions are consistent and controlled. Here's how you can manage the variables:

Use temperature-controlled devices: For precise fermentation, devices like yogurt makers and fermentation crocks are invaluable. These tools provide steady heat or cool conditions, ensuring your ferments develop properly. You can also place jars in a cool room, like a basement or a cupboard, that has a constant, moderate temperature. For smaller batches, consider using fermentation wraps that help insulate your jars and keep them warm.

Monitor your ferments regularly: While fermentation is a hands-off process, it's important to check in on your ferments. Burp jars (open and release any accumulated gas) periodically to avoid buildup, especially with ferments like kombucha or sauerkraut. If you're fermenting at home without specialized tools, use pH strips or a refractometer to test the acidity or sugar levels to gauge the fermentation progress.

Keep your ferments in a consistent environment: Light and temperature fluctuations can affect the rate of fermentation, so it's vital to store your ferments in a dark and stable environment. Light can interfere with bacterial growth, especially for ferments that rely on anaerobic (no oxygen) conditions, like lacto-fermentation.

The importance of maintaining the correct temperature throughout the fermentation process cannot be overstated. Consistent conditions will give you predictable results, allowing the beneficial bacteria to do their work, leading to flavorful, healthy ferments that can last for months.

Myths of Fermentation

Fermentation can seem like an intimidating process to newcomers, especially with all the misconceptions floating around. In reality, it's a safe, accessible, and rewarding method of preserving food, offering a burst of unique flavors, and providing health benefits. Unfortunately, many myths about fermentation can make it seem more complicated or risky than it actually is. Let's clear up some of the most common misconceptions so you can dive into the world of fermentation with confidence.

MYTH #1: FERMENTED FOOD IS ROTTEN FOOD

One of the biggest myths surrounding fermentation is the misconception that fermented food is simply spoiled or rotting food. In reality, fermentation is a controlled process that encourages the growth of beneficial microorganisms such as bacteria and yeasts, which preserve the food while enhancing its flavor. When you ferment food, you are encouraging the growth of **good bacteria**, not allowing the food to spoil. These bacteria are the same ones that help with digestion and gut health. Fermented foods are *alive* with beneficial bacteria, which is what makes them not only safe to eat but also incredibly nutritious. Unlike spoiled food, which is harmful and inedible, fermented foods are safe and packed with probiotics that contribute to overall health.

MYTH #2: BACTERIA ARE BAD

Another common myth is the fear of bacteria in food. Many people associate bacteria with illness and contamination, but the truth is that not all bacteria are harmful. In fact, many bacteria are beneficial for our health. The bacteria used in fermentation are known as **lactic acid bacteria** and they play a crucial role in the fermentation process. These bacteria help to break down sugars and produce acids, which preserve the food and give it its distinctive tangy flavor. They also contribute to gut health by promoting a healthy balance of microorganisms in the digestive system. So, rather than being a cause for concern, the bacteria in fermented foods are actually doing a lot of good for your body!

MYTH #3: FERMENTATION IS AN EXACT SCIENCE

While it's true that some precision is required, the idea that fermentation must be an exact science is a myth. One of the most beautiful aspects of fermentation is its flexibility. Fermentation is not an exact science, it's more of an art. You don't need to be a professional or have all the perfect conditions to successfully ferment food. Fermentation is influenced by factors like temperature, time, and the specific environment in which the food is fermenting, but it doesn't have to be strictly controlled for it to work. In fact, many traditional fermentation methods are passed down from generation to generation with very little precision involved. It's about finding the right balance that works for you and your tastes, experimenting, and adjusting as you go.

MYTH #4: FERMENTATION NEEDS A STARTER CULTURE

While some ferments, like yogurt or kombucha, do require a starter culture to kickstart the fermentation process, not all fermented foods need a starter. Many vegetable ferments, like sauerkraut, kimchi, and pickles, rely on **wild fermentation**, which means they use the naturally occurring bacteria and yeasts present on the vegetables themselves. This is why it's important to use fresh, high-quality ingredients when fermenting. The natural bacteria present in the environment, especially on the skins of fruits and vegetables, will be enough to get the fermentation process started. Starter cultures may speed up the process or help ensure consistency, but they are by no means necessary for successful fermentation.

MYTH #5: FERMENTATION IS A FAD

Fermentation is far from a passing trend. It's an ancient preservation method that has been used for thousands of years across cultures around the world. The popularity of fermentation may have grown recently, especially with the rise of health trends and gut health awareness, but the process itself is anything but new. From ancient civilizations in Mesopotamia and Egypt to modern-day Korea with its iconic kimchi, fermentation has been a key part of human food culture. The health benefits of fermented foods, especially their role in promoting a healthy gut microbiome, are being rediscovered, but fermentation has always been with us. It's not a fad, it's a time-honored tradition that's stood the test of time.

MYTH #6: FERMENTED FOODS ARE A LUXURY

Many people believe that fermented foods are expensive or require a lot of specialized equipment, but in reality, fermenting your own food at home is cost-effective and accessible. The ingredients for fermentation such as vegetables, fruits, salt, and water are often inexpensive and easy to find. Even if you're new to fermentation, you don't need specialized equipment to get started. A mason jar and some patience are all you really need for most ferments. The idea that fermented foods are a luxury is simply not truehome fermenting is an affordable and rewarding way to add healthy, probiotic-rich foods to your diet. Plus, you get to experiment and customize your ferments to your tastes, all while saving money compared to buying store-bought versions.

MYTH #7: FERMENTED FOOD CAN'T BE MADE AT HOME

It's often assumed that making fermented foods requires professional equipment, special training, or a "magic touch," but that's simply not the case. **Home fermentation** is both easy and accessible for beginners. You don't need a lab or advanced knowledge of science to ferment foods at home. With just a few simple tools, mason jars, a clean cloth, and some fresh vegetables you can start fermenting your own foods. Fermenting at home allows you to control the ingredients, customize flavors, and experiment without relying on the mass-produced, overly processed options found in stores.

MYTH #8: FERMENTED FOOD ALWAYS HAS A STRONG TASTE

Fermented foods don't always have to be overpoweringly sour or strong in flavor. The fermentation process can result in varying levels of sourness, and you can adjust the timing to your preference. If you like a milder flavor, you can ferment the food for a shorter period. If you prefer a stronger, more sour taste, you can let the food ferment for a longer time. Fermentation is about finding the right balance for your taste buds. And if you're new to fermenting, you can start with less tangy options like quick pickles or lightly fermented vegetables and gradually work your way up to more robust flavors like kimchi and sourdough.

Types of Fermentation Cultures

Fermentation can be achieved using two primary methods: wild fermentation and starter cultures. Both methods have their benefits and unique characteristics, so it's important to understand the difference to choose the one that best fits your needs.

Wild Fermentation relies on naturally occurring bacteria and yeasts found on the food itself or in the environment. For example, when fermenting cabbage to make sauerkraut, the lactic acid bacteria (LAB) are already present on the cabbage leaves and in the air. In this case, the food itself acts as the "starter culture," and all that's needed is time and the right conditions for fermentation. Wild fermentation is particularly popular for making kimchi, sauerkraut, and other vegetable ferments.

Starter Cultures are specific strains of bacteria or yeasts that are introduced into the fermentation process to ensure consistent and controlled fermentation. Common starter cultures include whey (used in yogurt and kefir), kombucha SCOBY (Symbiotic Culture of Bacteria and Yeast), and sauerkraut starter cultures. These cultures are purchased and added to the food to encourage specific microbial growth, and they can often speed up fermentation or ensure more predictable results. Starter cultures are particularly helpful when you want to ferment large batches of food or when you're aiming for very specific flavors or textures, such as the creamy consistency of yogurt.

Whey is one of the most commonly used starter cultures in fermentation. It's rich in lactic acid bacteria, and it's the byproduct of straining yogurt or cheese. When added to vegetable ferments like pickles or sauerkraut, whey helps jump-start the fermentation process by introducing a reliable source of beneficial bacteria.

Kombucha SCOBYs are used in the fermentation of sweet tea to make kombucha. A SCOBY (Symbiotic Culture of Bacteria and Yeast) contains both bacteria and yeast that work together to ferment the sugars in the tea, creating a tangy and effervescent beverage. The SCOBY acts as a starter culture for subsequent batches of kombucha, which is why it's important to always keep a healthy SCOBY on hand for continuous fermentation.

Both wild fermentation and starter cultures have their place in the world of fermentation. Wild fermentation gives you a more authentic, unpredictable, and spontaneous process, while starter cultures offer more control and consistency. Regardless of which method you choose, understanding the role of bacteria and yeast is fundamental to successful fermentation.

Probiotic Foods and Their Health Benefits

Incorporating fermented foods into your diet offers a multitude of health benefits, particularly when it comes to supporting digestive health. One of the most significant advantages is the presence of probiotics, live microorganisms that are essential for maintaining a healthy balance of bacteria in the gut. These "good" bacteria help to crowd out harmful bacteria and other pathogens, promoting optimal digestion, boosting nutrient absorption, and ensuring that your digestive system functions at its best.

Probiotics play an essential role in the breakdown of food, helping to digest complex compounds that may otherwise be difficult for the body to process. They also enhance the absorption of nutrients, ensuring that vitamins, minerals, and other beneficial compounds from your food are fully utilized by your body. This process is particularly important for those with compromised gut health or conditions like irritable bowel syndrome (IBS), as probiotics can help restore balance in the gut microbiota and alleviate digestive discomfort.

Beyond digestive health, probiotic-rich foods contribute to a strong immune system. A significant portion of the immune system is housed within the gut, and maintaining a healthy gut flora is crucial for supporting immune function. Probiotics stimulate the production of immune cells and antibodies, enhancing your body's ability to fight off infections. The presence of beneficial bacteria also helps reduce inflammation in the body, which is associated with numerous chronic conditions, including heart disease and autoimmune disorders.

What makes fermented foods particularly special is their impact on mental health. Research has increasingly shown a connection between gut health and brain health, often referred to as the "gut-brain axis." The beneficial bacteria in probiotics help produce neurotransmitters like serotonin and dopamine, which regulate mood and emotions. Fermented foods, therefore, may help improve mood, reduce stress, and even decrease symptoms of anxiety and depression. This connection makes probiotics not only beneficial for digestion but also an essential tool for mental well-being.

Sauerkraut and kimchi are two prime examples of fermented foods that are packed with probiotics. While both are made from cabbage, the flavor profiles and added benefits are quite distinct. Sauerkraut, with its milder, more subtle tang, is often enjoyed as a side dish or topping for meats, offering a light, refreshing crunch. In contrast, kimchi has a more robust and spicy flavor, thanks to the inclusion of chili peppers, garlic, and ginger, and it's a staple in many Korean dishes. Despite the differences in taste, both are excellent sources of probiotics, and they can be enjoyed in a variety of ways to suit different palates.

The fermentation process not only enhances the flavor of these foods but also makes them more nutritious. One of the key benefits of fermentation is the increased bioavailability of certain nutrients. Fermentation breaks down compounds that can inhibit the absorption of minerals like iron and zinc, making these nutrients more accessible to your body. For example, fermented cabbage in sauerkraut is easier for the body to digest, and the process increases the levels of B vitamins such as folate, which are essential for energy production and cellular health.

Moreover, fermenting vegetables and fruits often increases their fiber content, as the breakdown of starches and sugars during fermentation creates new fiber-like compounds that support gut health. This makes fermented foods a double benefit, providing both prebiotics (the food for good bacteria) and probiotics (the good bacteria themselves), ensuring your gut has the nourishment it needs to stay healthy.

Fermentation also has a protective role in the preservation of foods, as the process naturally creates an acidic environment, which helps prevent spoilage and the growth of harmful microorganisms. Unlike canned or pasteurized foods, which often lose their beneficial enzymes and bacteria during processing, fermented foods retain their living cultures, making them a living food that can continue to support gut health long after consumption.

Whether you choose to enjoy sauerkraut with your meal, mix some kimchi into a stir-fry, or drink a glass of kombucha, you're providing your body with a healthy dose of probiotics and nutrients. These foods not only add complex flavors to your dishes but also improve the health of your gut and immune system while supporting your mental well-being.

Starting with Simple Ferments like Sauerkraut and Kimchi

Fermentation can seem intimidating, but starting with simple recipes like sauerkraut and kimchi is a great way to learn. Sauerkraut is an excellent beginner ferment because it requires minimal ingredients and is easy to make. Kimchi, while a bit more complex due to its mix of spices and additional vegetables, is still accessible for those looking to dive deeper into fermentation.

Sauerkraut only requires cabbage, salt, and time, allowing the natural bacteria on the cabbage leaves to ferment and preserve the vegetables. The process is simple: you shred the cabbage, massage it with salt, and allow it to sit until it ferments into a tangy, probiotic-packed food.

Kimchi, on the other hand, adds layers of flavor through chili, garlic, ginger, and other spices. While it does take a bit more time and attention, it's still a straightforward recipe. We'll delve into the full kimchi recipe in Chapter 6, where we explore more advanced fermentation techniques.

Homemade Sauerkraut: A Classic Fermented Dish

Sauerkraut is one of the simplest and most rewarding fermented foods you can make at home. It requires just a few ingredients, and the result is a flavorful, tangy, and probiotic-rich food that can be used in a variety of dishes, from sandwiches to soups.

Ingredients:

- 1 small red or green cabbage (about 2 lbs)
- 1 tablespoon fine grind salt
- 1 teaspoon whole spices, such as caraway, dill, or celery seed (optional)

Instructions:

Begin by rinsing your cabbage and discarding any blemished leaves. Set aside one whole leaf to use later. Cut the cabbage into quarters, removing and discarding the core. Then, slice each quarter into thin strips to shred the cabbage.

Transfer the shredded cabbage into a large bowl, sprinkling the salt over it as you go. If using spices, sprinkle them in as well. With your hands or a large spoon, toss the cabbage to evenly distribute the salt, then massage the cabbage for a few minutes to help release its juice. Once the cabbage has wilted, continue to pound it down with a pickle packer or a large spoon to further release the liquid. This process will take several minutes, but the goal is to have the cabbage become juicy and submerged in its own brine.

Once the cabbage is sufficiently mashed and juicy, transfer it into a clean, sterilized mason jar. Pack it down firmly, ensuring the brine rises above the cabbage. You may need to add more cabbage and continue pressing until the jar is nearly full but not overstuffed. If you have extra cabbage, it makes a great fresh salad when tossed with a bit of olive oil.

Next, take the reserved cabbage leaf and cut it to the size of the jar opening. Lay it flat over the shredded cabbage to help keep the cabbage submerged. Add a Pickle Pebble or a clean weight on top to ensure the cabbage stays beneath the brine. Seal the jar with a Pickle Pipe or a regular lid, then label the jar with the date.

Store the jar in a cool, dark place to ferment. Check on it after a day or two if the cabbage hasn't released enough juice to cover itself, prepare a brine by dissolving 1/2 teaspoon salt in 1/2 cup water and pour it into the jar until the cabbage is fully submerged.

Fermentation will begin in a couple of days. Over the next 2–3 weeks (or longer, depending on your climate), you'll notice the cabbage swelling, developing gas pockets, and changing color. Bubbles, foam, and a sulfurous aroma are all normal signs of healthy fermentation.

Taste your sauerkraut after about 2–3 weeks. Once it has reached a tangy flavor and the cabbage is translucent, transfer the jar to the fridge to slow down the fermentation process. Sauerkraut can last for several months when stored in the refrigerator.

Garlicky Sauerkraut: A Bold Twist on a Classic

Garlic and cabbage are a timeless combination that brings a robust and aromatic twist to traditional sauerkraut. This garlic-infused version brings a punchy depth to the classic sauerkraut flavor, making it a perfect accompaniment to meats, sandwiches, or even as a snack on its own. The natural fermentation process of sauerkraut enhances the garlic's savory notes, giving it a tangy, probiotic-rich flavor that improves with time.

Ingredients

- 2 medium heads cabbage
- 5 whole garlic cloves, peeled and crushed
- 1-3 tablespoons sea salt

Instructions

Start by removing the outer leaves from the cabbage heads, setting aside one large leaf to use later. Discard the remaining leaves. Cut out the core of each cabbage head and rinse the cabbage thoroughly. Drain it well, then slice the cabbage into very thin ribbons.

Place the shredded cabbage into a large glass bowl. Add the crushed garlic cloves and sprinkle the salt over the cabbage. Mix everything thoroughly to ensure the salt and garlic are evenly distributed. Using a pounding tool or your hands, pound the cabbage mixture for about 3-5 minutes to help release the cabbage's natural juices. Cover the bowl with a clean kitchen towel and let it sit for 30 minutes, occasionally pounding it to help the fermentation process.

Once the cabbage has softened and released more liquid, transfer it into a sterilized mason jar. Press the cabbage mixture down, ensuring it is packed tightly. Place the reserved cabbage leaf on top of the cabbage, and then weigh it down with a fermenting weight to keep the cabbage submerged in its own juices. Cover the jar with a clean cloth, securing it with a rubber band or string to allow air to circulate while keeping dust and debris out.

Leave the jar at room temperature (ideally around 60-70°F) for 1-3 weeks to ferment. Make sure to check the jar daily to "burp" it, releasing any built-up pressure. If the cabbage is not fully submerged in the brine within 24 hours, dissolve 1 teaspoon of salt in 1 cup of water and add it to the jar to ensure the cabbage stays covered. After the fermentation period, skim off any scum that may have formed on top.

Once the sauerkraut has fermented to your liking, transfer it to the refrigerator where it can be stored for 2-3 months. The longer it ferments, the stronger and tangier the flavor will become, making it a wonderfully bold and probiotic-rich condiment.

Carrot & Ginger Sauerkraut: A Sweet and Spicy Kick

For a vibrant and flavor-packed variation of sauerkraut, try adding carrots and ginger to the mix. The sweetness of the carrots and the zing of fresh ginger bring an exciting twist to the traditional sauerkraut, creating a tangy and spicy flavor that pairs well with a variety of dishes. The bright colors and aromatic qualities of this fermented dish will add an extra dimension to your fermentation repertoire.

Ingredients

- 1 (2-3 pound) head green cabbage
- 2-3 carrots, peeled and grated
- 2-3 garlic cloves, peeled and finely minced
- 2-inch piece fresh ginger root, peeled and finely minced
- 1 tablespoon iodine-free salt

Instructions

Start by removing the outer leaves from the cabbage head, setting aside one large leaf to use later. Discard the other leaves. Cut out the core of the cabbage and rinse it well, ensuring it is clean and free of any dirt. Drain the cabbage head thoroughly, then shred it finely.

In a large bowl, combine the shredded cabbage, grated carrots, minced garlic, minced ginger, and salt. Mix everything together well to ensure an even distribution of salt and spices. Let the mixture sit for 30-60 minutes, allowing the salt to draw out the water from the vegetables.

Once the vegetables have softened, use your hands to massage the mixture for 2-5 minutes, helping release even more liquid and breaking down the cabbage further. Transfer the cabbage mixture into a sterilized mason jar, packing it down firmly. As you pack the jar, the liquid should rise to cover the vegetables. If not, add a bit of salted water (1 teaspoon salt dissolved in 1 cup of water) to ensure the vegetables remain submerged.

Place the reserved cabbage leaf on top of the mixture, then press down with a fermenting weight to keep the cabbage submerged. Cover the jar with a clean cloth and secure it with a rubber band or string to keep the air circulating. Leave the jar in a cool, dark place for 1-4 weeks to ferment. As with the garlicky sauerkraut, burp the jar daily to release excess gas and check for scum on the surface. If necessary, skim it off.

Once the sauerkraut reaches your desired level of fermentation, transfer it to the refrigerator. This version of sauerkraut will be good for 2-3 months, with the flavors deepening as it ages. The combination of sweet carrots and aromatic ginger gives this sauerkraut a unique twist that will elevate any meal.

The Science Behind Fermentation

Understanding the science behind fermentation can truly elevate your pickling and fermenting skills. The core of fermentation lies in the bacteria, yeasts, and molds that break down sugars in food, producing organic acids, alcohol, and gases as byproducts. In vegetable fermentation, naturally occurring lactic acid bacteria thrive in a saltwater environment. These bacteria consume the sugars in the vegetables, converting them into lactic acid, which acts as both a preservative and a flavor enhancer. This process not only preserves the food but also improves its digestibility, making fermented vegetables like sauerkraut and kimchi easier to absorb.

As the bacteria work, they produce lactic acid, lowering the pH of the food and creating an environment where harmful bacteria cannot survive. This acidic environment helps preserve the food while promoting the growth of beneficial bacteria, which contributes to the food's characteristic tangy flavor. The longer the fermentation process, the more pronounced the sourness, and the more complex the flavor profile becomes. The beauty of fermentation is that it doesn't just preserve food, it transforms it into something richer in flavor, nutrients, and beneficial compounds like B vitamins, enzymes, and antioxidants.

But fermentation doesn't just apply to vegetables. One of the fascinating aspects of fermentation is its versatility across food types. For example, fermented dairy foods such as buttermilk and cultured butter undergo similar processes, but they offer different textures and flavors. The fermentation of dairy products involves the action of specific bacteria that convert lactose into lactic acid. For example, buttermilk is produced by fermenting cream or milk with lactic acid bacteria, resulting in a tangy flavor. Cultured butter, on the other hand, is made by churning cream that has been inoculated with bacterial cultures, producing a rich, tangy butter with a smooth texture.

Fermented dairy recipes like buttermilk and cultured butter are wonderful additions to your fermenting repertoire. They follow the same principles of fermentation but provide a whole new level of flavor and texture to enjoy. These dairy ferments can be used in cooking or baking, adding complexity to your dishes.

Fermentation is a natural, powerful process that not only preserves food but also transforms it into something even more flavorful and healthful. Whether you're making simple fermented vegetables like sauerkraut or more complex dairy ferments like buttermilk and cultured butter, the key is to experiment and understand how the bacteria work to change the food over time. With each new batch, you'll not only develop your skills but also deepen your understanding of this ancient, healthful practice. In the next chapter, we'll dive deeper into kimchi, exploring more advanced fermentation techniques and providing you with a complete recipe.

Buttermilk

Buttermilk is a simple, tangy dairy product made by fermenting milk with a starter culture. It's perfect for use in baking, cooking, or even as a refreshing drink. Making your own buttermilk at home is incredibly easy and adds a depth of flavor that store-bought versions can't replicate.

Ingredients:

4 cups whole milk

1/8 tsp mesophilic starter culture (or you can use 2 tablespoons of plain yogurt as an alternative)

Instructions:

To make buttermilk, start by pouring 4 cups of whole milk into a clean mason jar. Add 1/8 teaspoon of mesophilic starter culture, or if you prefer a simpler alternative, you can use 2 tablespoons of plain yogurt. Stir the mixture gently to combine the ingredients. Cover the jar with a piece of cheesecloth, securing it with a rubber band or string, and leave it in a warm spot for 12–24 hours. This allows the milk to ferment, giving it a tangy flavor.

Once the fermentation is complete, place the jar in the refrigerator for at least 8 hours to firm up the buttermilk. After refrigeration, give the buttermilk a gentle stir to combine the liquid. It's now ready to use! This homemade buttermilk can be enjoyed on its own or used in various recipes for baking, cooking, or even as a drink.

Cultured Butter

Making cultured butter at home involves combining cream and yogurt to start the fermentation process, resulting in a rich, flavorful butter that's perfect for spreading. The process may seem intricate, but it's incredibly rewarding, and the final product is well worth the effort.

Ingredients:

- 8 cups good-quality heavy cream
- 1 cup plain whole milk yogurt
- 1/2 tsp fine sea salt

Instructions:

Start by blending 8 cups of good-quality heavy cream and 1 cup of plain whole milk yogurt in a large mason jar. Stir the ingredients gently to combine. Once mixed, seal the jar tightly and shake it vigorously for a minute to ensure everything is well incorporated. Cover the jar with a clean kitchen towel and place it in a warm location for 18–36 hours. This allows the cultures to ferment the cream, which thickens and develops a slightly tangy flavor.

After the fermentation period, seal the jar tightly and refrigerate it for 1–2 hours. Once chilled, line a fine-mesh sieve with a double layer of cheesecloth and set it over a large bowl. Pour the thickened cream mixture into a clean food processor and pulse on high speed. You will begin to see the yellow butter curds separating from the buttermilk. Slowly pour the buttermilk through the sieve, collecting the curds in the cloth. Discard the buttermilk or save it for other recipes.

Next, gather the cheesecloth around the butter curds and twist it tightly to press out any remaining buttermilk. Place the butter onto a clean kitchen towel and gently pat it to remove any excess moisture. Knead the butter a few times by hand, then pat dry again with the towel. Sprinkle the butter with 1/2 teaspoon of fine sea salt and knead it in to ensure the salt is evenly distributed. Finally, shape the butter into a log using parchment paper, roll it up, and twist the ends to seal. Refrigerate the butter until ready to use.

Chapter 6
Fermentation Techniques and Recipes for Beginners

Fermentation opens up a world of possibilities when it comes to creating rich, flavorful, and health-boosting foods. While sauerkraut is a great introduction to fermentation, there's a whole range of other fermented foods that are equally rewarding and flavorful. In this chapter, we will take a deeper dive into more advanced fermentation techniques, including how to make kimchi from scratch, brewing your own kombucha, creating fermented hot sauce, and preparing fermented garlic. These are all excellent projects for beginner fermenters looking to build their skills and try something new in the kitchen.

How to Make Kimchi from Scratch: A Beginner's Guide

Kimchi is a spicy, tangy, and probiotic-rich fermented dish that has been a staple in Korean cuisine for centuries. This recipe offers a simple yet delicious way to make kimchi at home, giving you full control over the spice level and flavor. With a balance of gochugaru (Korean chili flakes), garlic, ginger, and a touch of fish sauce, this kimchi will develop its bold flavors over time and can be enjoyed as a side dish or added to various meals.

Ingredients:

- 1 napa cabbage (about 3 pounds)
- 2 ½ tablespoons (42g) fine sea salt
- 12 green onions, trimmed and cut into 2-inch pieces
- 2 tablespoons rice thickener (recipe below)
- 5 tablespoons (45g) gochugaru (Korean red chili pepper powder)
- 8 cloves garlic, finely grated

- 1 (2-inch) knob fresh ginger, finely grated
- 2 tablespoons fish sauce (or a vegan alternative such as miso paste)
- 4 teaspoons sugar
- 2 tablespoons water

Rice Thickener:

- 1 tablespoon sweet rice flour
- ½ cup cold water

Instructions:

Start by cutting the napa cabbage in half lengthwise, removing the core, and slicing it into 1 ½-inch pieces. Trim the root ends of the green onions, slice them in half lengthwise, and cut them into 2-inch pieces. Place the cabbage and green onions in a large bowl, sprinkle with salt, and toss well. Cover with a towel and let sit for 1–2 hours, tossing occasionally. Once wilted, rinse the cabbage well under cold water and set it aside to drain for 20–30 minutes.

While the cabbage is wilting, make the rice thickener by combining rice flour and cold water in a saucepan, heating until it forms a thick paste. Let it cool. Next, mix the gochugaru, garlic, ginger, fish sauce (or miso for a vegan version), sugar, and water in a separate bowl. Add the cooled rice thickener and stir until well combined.

Once the cabbage is ready, massage the chili paste into the cabbage and green onions using gloves. Pack the mixture into sterilized mason jars, pressing it down firmly to release the brine. Leave about 1 inch of space at the top. Seal the jar and let it ferment in a cool, dark place. After 1–2 days, "burp" the jar by pressing down on the cabbage to release any gas buildup. Taste the kimchi after 3–5 days and refrigerate once it reaches the desired level of tanginess.

Tips for Customizing Your Kimchi:

Spicy Kimchi: If you prefer a spicier kimchi, increase the amount of gochugaru or use a hotter variety of chili flakes.

Vegan Kimchi: Omit the fish sauce and substitute with miso paste or another vegan-friendly umami flavoring.

Adding Vegetables: Kimchi is versatile, and you can experiment with adding vegetables like radishes, carrots, or even daikon to change up the texture and flavor.

This recipe will yield about 1 quart of delicious, homemade kimchi that's rich in probiotics and perfect for adding a spicy, tangy kick to any meal.

Fermented Hot Sauce: Homemade with a Kick

If you love spice and flavor, homemade fermented hot sauce is a great way to add a kick to your meals. Fermenting hot sauce not only deepens the flavor, but it also adds probiotics to your sauce, making it a gut-friendly condiment. With just a few ingredients, you can create a custom hot sauce that has a depth of flavor you can't get from store-bought varieties.

Ingredients:

- 1 pound red serrano peppers (or any chili peppers of your choice), stems removed
- 1 quart unchlorinated water
- 3 tablespoons sea salt (do not use iodized salt)
- ½–1 cup white wine vinegar (to taste, use good quality vinegar for better flavor)

Instructions:

Start by roughly chopping the serrano peppers and packing them into a clean mason jar, leaving about 1 inch of headspace at the top. As the peppers ferment, they may rise slightly, so ensure there is room for expansion.

In a separate container, mix the unchlorinated water and sea salt until the salt is fully dissolved. Pour enough brine over the peppers to cover them completely. You may need to press the peppers down a bit to ensure they stay submerged. It's crucial to keep the peppers under the brine to prevent spoilage. "Burp" the jar every day by slightly unscrewing the lid to let out any accumulating gas.

Seal the jar and store it in a cool, dark place away from direct sunlight, ideally between 55-75°F (13-24°C). Let the peppers ferment for at least 1 week. The fermentation process will be most active during the first 1–2 weeks. The brine will turn cloudy, and the peppers will develop a tangy, acidic flavor as fermentation progresses.

After 1–2 weeks, drain the peppers, but save some of the brine. Add the fermented peppers to a food processor or blender, and blend with ½ cup of the reserved brine and ½ cup of vinegar. Adjust the amount of brine or vinegar to your taste preference, more brine will add a saltier flavor, while more vinegar will make the sauce more acidic.

For a smoother sauce, strain the mixture to remove solids, or leave it as-is for a thicker texture. If desired, you can cook the sauce by transferring it to a pot, bringing it to a quick boil, and simmering for 15 minutes. This step will halt the fermentation process and blend the flavors together, but it will remove the probiotic benefits.

Once the hot sauce is ready, pour it into bottles or jars and store it in the refrigerator. It can last for months, but be aware that fermentation might continue in the fridge, causing pressure to build in sealed bottles. If you don't cook the sauce, "burp" the bottles occasionally to release gas buildup.

Notes:

The pH of this hot sauce is approximately 3.7, which is safe for refrigeration. However, if you plan on storing it long-term in sealed bottles, you may want to consider water-bath canning to further preserve it and prevent any potential issues.

If you prefer a spicier hot sauce, feel free to experiment with hotter peppers or increase the amount of chili flakes to suit your taste. The beauty of homemade hot sauce is the ability to tailor the heat level to your liking.

For a vegan version of this fermented hot sauce, simply omit the fish sauce and substitute it with miso or soy sauce to provide the same savory, umami flavor without animal products.

Kombucha: Brewing Your Own Probiotic Beverage

Kombucha is a fermented tea that has gained popularity for its health benefits, including its probiotic content and digestive support. Making kombucha at home is a fun and rewarding process that allows you to customize the flavor and adjust the sweetness to your liking. While the process takes longer than some other ferments, the result is a refreshing, naturally carbonated drink.

Ingredients:

- 4–6 tea bags (black or green tea)
- 1 cup sugar (white or cane)
- 1 SCOBY (Symbiotic Culture of Bacteria and Yeast)

1 gallon filtered water

Instructions:

Begin by boiling 1 gallon of filtered water. Once the water reaches a boil, steep the tea bags in the hot water for 10–15 minutes, depending on how strong you want the tea to be. Remove the tea bags and add the sugar, stirring until it's fully dissolved. Allow the sweetened tea to cool to room temperature.

Once cooled, pour the sweetened tea into a clean glass jar or brewing vessel. Add the SCOBY to the jar along with any starter liquid that came with it (this helps to establish the right environment for fermentation). Cover the jar with a cloth or coffee filter, secured with a rubber band, to allow air to flow in while keeping contaminants out.

Let the kombucha ferment at room temperature for 7–14 days, depending on your taste preference. The longer it ferments, the more sour it will become. After a week, start tasting it to see if it has reached your preferred flavor. When the kombucha is ready, remove the SCOBY and set it aside with some of the liquid to start your next batch.

You can now bottle the kombucha and refrigerate it. If you like, you can add flavorings like ginger, berries, or herbs before bottling to create your own custom kombucha.

Fermented Garlic: A Robust Addition to Any Dish

Fermented garlic offers a mild, sweet flavor that enhances everything from sauces to salads. The fermentation process softens the sharpness of raw garlic, creating a rich, savory addition to many meals. Fermenting garlic is easy and only requires a few ingredients, but it takes some patience as the flavor continues to develop over time.

Ingredients:

- 3 cups peeled garlic cloves
- 1 tablespoon salt
- Water to fill the jar

Instructions:

Start by packing the peeled garlic cloves into a clean, quart-sized mason jar. Add the salt to the jar, then fill the jar with water, ensuring the garlic is completely submerged. It's important to keep the garlic fully covered to prevent exposure to air, which can lead to spoilage.

Cap the jar and leave it to ferment at room temperature for 3–5 days. During this time, "burp" the jar at least once every 24 hours by loosening the lid to release any gas buildup. This step is essential to prevent pressure from building up in the jar.

Once the fermentation process is complete and the garlic has developed a tangy, slightly sour flavor, store it in the refrigerator. The fermented garlic can be used just like fresh garlic, adding depth and flavor to your favorite dishes. It will keep in the fridge for several weeks.

Ginger Beer: A Refreshing, Naturally Fermented Beverage

Ginger Beer is a fun and flavorful homemade ferment that offers a probiotic-rich, fizzy drink. This recipe brings the heat of fresh ginger, combined with sugar and water, to create a naturally carbonated drink. As it ferments, it develops a balance of sweet and spicy flavors with a touch of effervescence. Perfect for sipping on hot summer days or adding to cocktails, this ginger beer is an easy and rewarding brew to make at home.

Ingredients:

- 10 cm of organic ginger (or more for extra gingery flavor)
- 750 ml + 1750 ml of water (left for 8 hours to allow chlorine to evaporate)
- 250 ml of sugar
- 150 ml of ginger bug liquid (or starter culture)

Instructions:

Start by feeding your ginger bug a day before you begin brewing. Leave it at room temperature outside of the fridge to activate. On the day of brewing, bring 750 ml of water to a boil in a large pot. Add the 10 cm of sliced ginger and simmer for about 20 minutes, allowing the ginger flavor to infuse into the water. You can add additional flavors at this stage, like berries or herbs, to customize your ginger beer. Once the ginger mixture has simmered, remove it from the heat and stir in the sugar, dissolving it completely. Let the mixture cool to room temperature because it's crucial to avoid killing the beneficial bacteria with heat.

After the mixture has cooled, combine it with the remaining 1750 ml of water, and stir. Now, vigorously stir your ginger bug to evenly distribute the live cultures throughout the liquid. Add approximately 150 ml of the ginger bug liquid to the sugar-ginger mixture and pour the entire contents into sterilized glass bottles, ensuring there's some room left at the top for expansion. Seal the bottles tightly and leave them at room temperature for the fermentation process to begin.

For the next 2 days, "burp" your bottles daily by opening and closing them quickly to release any built-up gas. After 3–5 days, the ginger beer will develop its characteristic fizz and flavor. Once you're happy with the level of fermentation, move the bottles to the fridge to stop the process. The ginger beer is ready to be enjoyed chilled. Keep in mind that since it's a fermented drink, it may contain a small amount of alcohol.

Sparkling Apple Water Kefir: A Probiotic-Rich, Refreshing Drink

Sparkling Apple Water Kefir is a light and tangy fermented beverage, perfect for those seeking a naturally carbonated drink with gut-friendly probiotics. Water kefir is a versatile ferment that can be flavored with fruits like apples, lemons, or berries to create your own signature sparkling beverages. This kefir water base, combined with the sweet apple juice, results in a refreshingly fizzy drink that's perfect for hydration and digestion.

Ingredients:

- 3 tbsp water kefir grains
- 1/2 lemon, cut into quarters
- 1 dried apricot
- 1 liter of filtered water
- 3 heaping tbsp sugar
- 250 ml apple juice (preferably fresh)

Instructions:

Start by dissolving the sugar into the water in a glass jug. Once the sugar is fully dissolved, rinse the water kefir grains under cold water and add them to the sugared water, along with the lemon quarters and dried apricot. Let this mixture ferment at room temperature for 24 hours. Afterward, strain the kefir water to remove the apricot and lemon quarters. Squeeze the juice from the lemon quarters back into the liquid before discarding them.

At this point, you can drink the kefir water as is or proceed with the secondary fermentation for a sparkling version. For secondary fermentation, transfer the kefir water to a sealable glass bottle, then add the apple juice. Seal the bottle tightly and leave it to ferment at room temperature for another 24 hours. Be cautious when opening the bottle after fermentation, as the natural carbonation can cause the liquid to overflow. Chill the kefir in the fridge for a few hours before enjoying a refreshing, probiotic-packed drink.

To store the kefir grains when not in use, submerge them in lightly sugared water with a dried apricot in the fridge until you're ready for the next batch

Fermented Lemons: A Tangy, Citrusy Delight for Your Kitchen

Fermented Lemons are a simple yet transformative addition to your kitchen staples. These tangy, salted lemons add a vibrant, citrusy kick to a variety of dishes, from stews to salads. The fermentation process enhances their flavor, making them a perfect condiment or garnish. This easy recipe requires minimal ingredients, and the results are a deeply flavored, preserved fruit that can last for months.

Ingredients:

- 2–3 unwaxed lemons
- 2–3 heaping teaspoons salt

Instructions:

Begin by slicing the lemons nearly in half, leaving a small portion of the lemon connected at the base to maintain the quarters intact. Make another crosswise cut so that the lemon can open up for stuffing with salt. Add about 1 teaspoon of salt into the cuts of each lemon. Pack the lemons into a clean jar, pressing them down with a pestle to release their juices. Continue packing the lemons tightly, ensuring they are submerged in their own juices. If necessary, use a clean rock or shot glass to weigh the lemons down, helping to keep them submerged and preventing mold from forming.

Seal the jar and store it in a dark, draft-free area, such as under the sink or in an airing cupboard, at room temperature for 3–4 weeks. During this time, you may need to "burp" the jar by slightly unscrewing the lid a couple of times a week to release any gas buildup. After the fermentation period, refrigerate the lemons. They'll last for about a week in the fridge once opened, but they're best used within a few days for maximum flavor.

Lacto-Fermented Cherry Tomatoes: A Burst of Flavor in Every Bite

Lacto-Fermented Cherry Tomatoes are an easy and flavorful way to preserve fresh tomatoes. The lactic acid fermentation process imparts a tangy flavor that enhances the natural sweetness of the tomatoes. These fermented tomatoes are perfect as a snack, in salads, or as an addition to savory dishes.

Ingredients:

- Enough cherry tomatoes to fill a quart jar
- 2 tablespoons of whey (or salt for non-dairy)
- 1 tablespoon sea salt
- Filtered water to cover

Instructions:

Fill a clean quart jar with washed cherry tomatoes, leaving about 1-1/2 inches of space from the rim. Add the whey and sea salt to the jar, then fill the jar with filtered water, leaving about 1-1/2 inches of headspace. Swirl the jar gently to mix the salt and whey into the water, then cover the jar tightly. Allow the tomatoes to ferment at room temperature for 3–4 days. During this time, be sure to "burp" the jar daily by opening the lid to release the gases that build up during fermentation.

Once the fermentation is complete, transfer the jar to cold storage in the fridge. The fermented cherry tomatoes are ready to enjoy and can be kept for several months, though they're most fresh and flavorful within the first few weeks. Enjoy them as a snack, in salads, or as a tangy addition to any dish.

Fermenting Sauces and Dressings: Elevating Your Meals with Probiotics

Fermented sauces and dressings add a unique depth of flavor to any dish, with the added benefit of gut-healthy probiotics. By fermenting your own condiments, you can transform everyday sauces into nutrient-rich, probiotic-packed powerhouses. Whether it's a spicy mustard, a tangy ketchup, or a zesty salad dressing, these fermented additions will enhance both the taste and the nutritional profile of your meals. What's more, the fermentation process not only intensifies the flavors but also introduces beneficial bacteria that support digestion and overall health.

In this section, we'll explore a variety of fermented sauces and dressings that can be easily incorporated into your kitchen. The best part? They're all incredibly customizable! You can adjust the ingredients to suit your taste whether you want a spicier kick, a smoother texture, or more vibrant herbs. These homemade creations are far superior to store-bought versions, as they are free of additives and preservatives, and packed with fresh, organic ingredients.

Fermented Mustard: A Tangy, Spicy Addition to Your Meals

Fermented mustard is a tangy, spicy condiment that adds a rich, fermented kick to sandwiches, burgers, and more. By fermenting mustard seeds with natural bacteria, you can enhance the flavor while also benefiting from the probiotics created during fermentation. This simple, yet powerful, recipe transforms mustard into a nutritious, probiotic-rich food that's just as great for your gut as it is for your taste buds.

Ingredients:

- 150g yellow mustard seeds
- 10g salt
- 25g fresh turmeric (or ½ tsp. turmeric powder)
- 1 clove minced garlic
- 310 - 375 ml water
- 1 teaspoon brine from a previous lacto-fermentation (or 1 pouch of commercial starter culture)

Instructions:

In a 500ml jar, combine the mustard seeds, salt, turmeric, garlic, and brine. Add enough water to fill the jar, and then close the jar tightly, installing the airlock. Let the mixture ferment at room temperature for 5 to 10 days. If you prefer a tangier mustard, let it ferment longer.

After the fermentation period, open the jar, filter the liquid, and set it aside. In a blender or food processor, blend the mustard seeds and the reserved liquid, gradually adding more liquid until you achieve your desired consistency. You can adjust the texture by adding water, cider vinegar, or white wine to enhance the flavor further.

Fermented Ketchup: Sweet, Tangy, and Probiotic-Rich

Fermented ketchup offers a probiotic-packed alternative to the store-bought version, adding richness and depth to any dish. With a base of tomato paste and natural sweeteners like maple syrup or raw honey, this ketchup balances the sweetness with tangy acidity, enhanced by the fermentation process.

Ingredients:

- 2 (6oz) cans of tomato paste or 1.5 cups homemade tomato paste
- 3 tablespoons maple syrup or raw honey
- 3 tablespoons raw vinegar (or homemade vinegar)
- 2 tablespoons whey or brine from existing vegetable ferments
- 1/4 teaspoon onion powder
- 1/2 teaspoon sea salt
- 1/8 teaspoon black pepper
- 1/8 teaspoon allspice

Instructions:

To make your fermented ketchup, combine all ingredients in a bowl, tasting and adjusting the seasonings as needed. Transfer the mixture to a pint-sized mason jar, fitting it with an airlock or regular lid. Allow the ketchup to sit at room temperature for 2-3 days, and be sure to "burp" the jar once or twice daily if using a regular lid to release any buildup of gas. If using an airlock, there's no need for this step.

After the fermentation period, transfer the ketchup to the fridge and allow it to chill for another 3 days. Your homemade ketchup is now ready to enjoy on burgers, fries, or roasted vegetables! It can be stored in the refrigerator for 3-6 months.

Fermented Salad Dressings: A Probiotic Twist on Your Favorite Vinaigrette

Fermented salad dressings are an excellent way to bring a tangy, probiotic boost to your salads while adding extra complexity to the flavor. By fermenting basic ingredients like lemon, garlic, and olive oil, you introduce beneficial bacteria into your diet in a way that's both delicious and nutritious. Here are two fermented salad dressing recipes to enhance your meals:

Probiotic Lemon-Garlic Salad Dressing Vinaigrette

Ingredients:

- 1/4 cup lemon juice (from 2-3 lemons)
- 3 to 4 cloves garlic, minced
- 3/4 cup extra virgin olive oil
- 1 teaspoon raw apple cider vinegar
- 1 small handful fresh parsley (or herbs of your choice)
- 1/2 teaspoon sea salt (or more to taste)
- 1/4 teaspoon ground black pepper

Instructions:

Combine all ingredients in a small jar and shake well to combine. For a probiotic boost, allow the dressing to sit at room temperature for 12-24 hours to ferment before using. This will allow the garlic and lemon to infuse the oil with tangy, fermented flavors. You can store it at room temperature for 4-5 days before it starts to sour. After that, move it to the refrigerator to extend its shelf life.

Kombucha Salad Dressing

This bright, tangy, probiotic-rich dressing is a versatile addition to your kitchen, bringing a refreshing flavor to salads, roasted vegetables, meats, and even as a dip for raw veggies. The natural acidity of kombucha blends beautifully with olive oil, herbs, garlic, and optional honey, creating a wholesome homemade dressing that's both flexible and deeply flavorful. Whether you prefer a classic mustard-honey vinaigrette or a herb-filled Italian-style dressing, this recipe can be customized to match your taste and whatever ingredients you have on hand.

Ingredients:

1 cup olive oil

1/2 cup kombucha

1 teaspoon salt (or onion/garlic salt for extra flavor)

2 tablespoons kombucha mustard (optional)

1/2–1 teaspoon onion powder or garlic powder

1/2 teaspoon dried herbs or 1 tablespoon fresh herbs (parsley, thyme, oregano, basil, etc.), finely chopped

2 cloves garlic, minced

1/4 teaspoon freshly ground black pepper

1 tablespoon raw honey (optional, for a sweeter dressing)

Instructions:

Combine the kombucha, salt, mustard, garlic, herbs, pepper, honey, and any spices you choose in a mixing bowl. Slowly drizzle in the olive oil while whisking, allowing the mixture to emulsify into a smooth, rich dressing. Adjust the herbs, sweetness, or seasonings to suit your taste. For a bolder flavor, let the dressing sit for an hour or more so the garlic and herbs can infuse into the kombucha and oil. Store in a sealed jar in the refrigerator and shake well before each use. This simple, flexible vinaigrette is perfect for dressing salads, drizzling over roasted vegetables, marinating meats, or adding a probiotic boost to everyday meals.

Chapter 7
Advancing Your Fermentation Skills

Fermentation is an art that goes beyond just preserving food; it transforms it into something uniquely flavorful, nutritious, and alive. As you gain more confidence with basic fermenting, it's time to explore advanced techniques that will help you create even more complex and unique flavors. In this chapter, we'll dive deeper into troubleshooting common fermentation problems, explore how to craft flavored kombucha, guide you through making homemade yogurt, and introduce advanced fermentation tools like airlock systems and fermentation crocks. Lastly, we'll explore **wild fermentation**, a process that allows you to craft artisan flavors using wild microorganisms.

Troubleshooting Common Fermentation Problems

As you advance in your fermentation journey, you may encounter a few hiccups along the way. Don't worry, most fermentation issues are easily fixable once you understand what might be causing them. Here are some common problems you might face, along with solutions to keep your ferments on track.

Mold Formation: If you see mold forming on the surface of your ferment, it's usually a sign that the vegetables were exposed to air. Ensure that your ferments remain fully submerged in the brine or liquid. You can use a fermentation weight, a clean stone, or even a cabbage leaf to help keep everything below the liquid surface. If mold appears, remove it carefully and check for any unpleasant smells, as mold can indicate contamination.

Off Smells or Spoilage: Fermentation should smell sour but pleasant, with some varieties having an earthy or tangy aroma. If the ferment has a rotten or off-putting smell, it could be a sign that it has spoiled. This can happen if there was not enough salt, or if the ferment was exposed to air too long. Always ensure proper sealing and check your recipe to ensure the correct salt ratio.

Fermentation Not Starting: Sometimes fermentation can be sluggish, especially if the temperature is too low. Fermentation thrives in warm temperatures (65–75°F). If your kitchen is cooler, try moving your ferments to a warmer spot or using a fermentation mat or temperature-controlled environment to encourage the process.

Too Salty or Too Sour: If your ferment tastes too salty or sour, the brine may need adjusting. You can dilute it with a bit of water or adjust your fermentation time to reduce the sourness. Tasting along the way can help you monitor the development of flavors and prevent over-fermentation.

With these troubleshooting tips in hand, you can confidently tackle any fermentation mishaps and continue improving your craft.

Blueberry Kombucha: A Fresh, Probiotic-Filled Beverage

Making your own flavored kombucha at home is a fun way to experiment with flavors and boost your gut health with every sip. This blueberry kombucha recipe adds a sweet, fruity twist to the already tangy, probiotic-rich drink, with the natural flavors of fresh blueberries and a touch of citrus or ginger for a refreshing finish. Here's a step-by-step guide to creating your own blueberry kombucha using homemade first-fermentation kombucha.

Ingredients:

½ gallon kombucha from a first fermentation (this is not store-bought kombucha, 1.9 L)

½ cup blueberries (fresh or frozen, 100 g)

½ cup water (120 mL)

1 Tbsp sugar (10 g)

Optional: 1 tsp lemon zest, small knob of fresh ginger

Instructions:

Start by combining the blueberries, water, and sugar in a medium saucepan. If you'd like to add a little extra zest, throw in some lemon zest and freshly minced ginger. Cook the mixture over medium heat, uncovered, until the berries burst and begin to mash slightly, creating a thick liquid. Allow the mixture to cool down to room temperature. To speed up the cooling process, you can place the pan in a sink full of cold water.

Once the blueberry mixture has cooled, transfer it into a large glass bowl or pitcher. Add your homemade first-fermentation kombucha and stir the two together, making sure the blueberry liquid is well mixed with the kombucha for a consistent flavor infusion.

Now it's time to bottle the kombucha. Carefully pour the kombucha mixture into fermentation bottles, leaving about 2 inches of space at the top of each bottle. Seal the bottles tightly to ensure no air can enter during fermentation.

Next, store the bottles in a dark place at room temperature. Let the kombucha ferment for 3 to 10 days, depending on the temperature of your environment. If you're in a warmer climate, the fermentation process will be quicker, while cooler environments may require more time. Taste the kombucha throughout the process to monitor its carbonation levels and decide when it's ready.

Once the kombucha has reached your preferred level of carbonation, strain out the blueberry pulp if desired, then refrigerate the beverage for a few hours. The kombucha will be ready to serve and can be stored in the fridge for up to several weeks in sealed bottles.

Flavoring Kombucha: Fruit and Spice Combinations

Here are a few popular combinations you can try, but feel free to get creative with your choices:

Strawberry and Basil: Add fresh strawberries and a few basil leaves for a refreshing herbal note that pairs beautifully with the natural tang of the kombucha.

Ginger-Lime: For a zesty, spicy kick, add a few slices of fresh ginger and a squeeze of lime juice to your kombucha.

Peach and Cinnamon: Fresh peaches paired with a cinnamon stick create a sweet and slightly spicy kombucha, perfect for summer.

Cranberry-Orange: Fresh cranberries and orange slices make for a tart and citrusy kombucha with a festive feel.

Cherry-Almond: Cherries and a dash of almond extract create a sweet, nutty flavor that's both unique and delicious.

You can also experiment with herbal flavors like mint, lavender, or chamomile for a more aromatic kombucha. For a spicy kick, try adding jalapeño slices or black pepper. The options are endless, so don't be afraid to try different fruits, herbs, and spices until you find your perfect kombucha blend.

Homemade Yogurt: The Perfect Fermented Dairy

Making homemade yogurt is a rewarding process that allows you to create creamy, probiotic-rich yogurt right in your own kitchen. The best part is, you can tailor the flavor and texture to your preference by adjusting the fermentation time.

Ingredients:

- 1 quart whole milk (or any milk of your choice)
- 2 tablespoons plain yogurt with live active cultures (this will act as your starter)

Instructions:

Heat the milk in a saucepan over medium heat until it reaches about 180°F (82°C). This step helps denature the proteins in the milk, ensuring a smooth and creamy texture. Once heated, let the milk cool to about 110°F (43°C), which is the ideal temperature for culturing.

Add the 2 tablespoons of plain yogurt to a small bowl. Slowly add some of the cooled milk to the yogurt, stirring to dissolve it. Then, pour the yogurt mixture back into the saucepan, stirring gently. Pour the milk and yogurt mixture into a clean jar or container, cover it with a lid or cloth, and place it in a warm environment, such as an oven with a light on, for 6–12 hours. The longer the fermentation, the thicker and tangier the yogurt will be.

Once your yogurt has fermented, transfer it to the refrigerator to chill for a few hours. Enjoy your homemade yogurt as-is, or add fresh fruit, honey, or granola for a delicious breakfast or snack.

Advanced Fermentation Techniques: Airlock Systems and Fermentation Crocks

As you progress in your fermentation journey, you may want to explore more advanced techniques to streamline your process and achieve better results. Two popular tools used by advanced fermenters are airlock systems and fermentation crocks.

Airlock Systems: An airlock system helps prevent oxygen from entering your ferment while allowing gases to escape. This is especially important for ferments like kombucha and beer, where you want to maintain an anaerobic (oxygen-free) environment for the beneficial bacteria to thrive. Using an airlock can prevent contamination and ensure consistent, successful ferments. It's especially useful for larger batches or fermenting in sealed containers.

Fermentation Crocks: A fermentation crock is a traditional vessel used for fermenting vegetables. These crocks typically have a water-sealed lid, which helps create an anaerobic environment while preventing air and mold from entering the ferment. The crock allows for larger quantities of ferments and is ideal for making sauerkraut, kimchi, or pickles. Fermentation crocks also provide a stable environment for long-term fermentation, which is especially important for larger batches.

Both airlock systems and fermentation crocks are designed to help you control the fermentation process more precisely, ensuring a better outcome with each batch.

Fermenting Meat: A Bold New Way to Add Flavor and Nutrition

Fermenting meat might sound unconventional, but it's a practice that has been used for centuries to preserve meat and develop complex flavors. When done correctly, fermented meats are not only delicious but can also be rich in probiotics and beneficial enzymes, promoting better digestion and gut health. While most people associate fermentation with vegetables or dairy products, fermenting meat is an ancient technique that continues to offer unique flavors and preservation benefits in modern kitchens.

The process of fermenting meat involves culturing the meat with specific bacterial strains that break down proteins and sugars, leading to the development of distinctive flavors and a preserved shelf life. This can be seen in fermented meats like salami, pepperoni, and other types of cured sausages. However, it's important to note that fermenting meat requires precision, as improper fermentation can lead to spoilage and health risks.

Fermenting meat involves several steps: first, you will need to choose high-quality cuts of meat, such as pork, beef, or poultry. These meats are usually mixed with salt, spices, and sometimes a fermentation culture, which encourages the growth of beneficial bacteria. The meat is then left to ferment at a controlled temperature, allowing the bacteria to break down proteins and create lactic acid, which preserves the meat.

One of the main challenges of fermenting meat is ensuring the proper temperature control. Meats need to be kept at a specific temperature range, typically between 55-65°Ffor the fermentation process to occur safely. If the temperature is too high, the meat may spoil, while too low a temperature can slow the fermentation process or stop it entirely.

Fermented meats are often smoked or dried after fermentation to add extra flavor and help with preservation. These steps further enhance the taste, creating a rich, savory product that is ready to be enjoyed in sandwiches, salads, or as an appetizer. Fermented meats are typically stored in a cool, dry place, and when done properly, they can last for months, providing a convenient and flavorful food source.

Wild Fermentation: Creating Artisan Flavors

Wild fermentation is the practice of allowing naturally occurring bacteria, yeast, and molds from the environment to ferment your food. This process differs from controlled fermentation, which relies on specific strains of bacteria or yeast. Wild fermentation embraces the microorganisms present in the air, on the food, and in the environment to create unique flavors that can vary from batch to batch.

To begin wild fermentation, you'll want to use high-quality ingredients that are free from pesticides, as the wild microorganisms on these ingredients will be vital to the fermentation process. For vegetables, choose those that are fresh and organic. For drinks like kombucha, make sure to use loose-leaf tea and natural sugar.

Wild fermentation allows you to experiment with different types of vegetables, fruits, and grains, resulting in unique flavors and textures. This technique can be used for a wide variety of ferments, including pickles, kimchi, sourdough bread, and even fermented beverages like wild fruit sodas.

Wild fermentation encourages creativity and experimentation. As you gain more experience, you'll develop an appreciation for the subtle complexities and nuances that come with each batch, creating artisan ferments that are truly one-of-a-kind.

By now, you've honed your fermentation skills and are ready to experiment with new techniques and flavors. Whether it's creating your own kombucha flavors, experimenting with advanced tools like airlocks and fermentation crocks, or delving into the world of wild fermentation, there are endless possibilities to explore. Keep practicing, troubleshooting, and trying new things, and you'll continue to refine your fermentation craft. In the next chapter, we'll explore even more advanced fermentation projects that will push your skills to new heights, so get ready to continue your journey into the world of fermented foods!

Chapter 8
Creating Your Signature Preserves and Ferments

Fermenting and pickling not only help preserve food but also allow you to get creative in the kitchen, developing your own signature flavors. As you become more comfortable with the basics of fermentation and preservation, you'll want to experiment with different ingredients, spices, and methods to personalize your creations. This chapter will guide you through personalizing your pickles, crafting artisan-style ferments, making your own vinegar, fermenting condiments like mustard and mayonnaise, and exploring the world of wild fermentation, where you allow nature to create the flavors for you.

Personalizing Your Pickles: Custom Spice Blends and Flavors

Pickles are an incredibly versatile preserve that can be customized to suit any taste. While the basic pickle brine made of vinegar, water, salt, and sugar forms the foundation, the real magic comes from the spices and flavorings you choose to add. Customizing your spice blend allows you to create unique, personalized pickles that will stand out in your pantry.

The process begins with selecting a base spice blend that suits the type of pickle you're making. A basic pickling spice mix often includes mustard seeds, coriander, black peppercorns, and dill. These provide a balanced flavor that complements a variety of vegetables. But the fun starts when you begin to experiment with additional spices and flavorings to tailor the pickles to your liking.

For a warming, slightly sweet flavor, consider adding cinnamon sticks, cloves, or allspice to the brine. These spices give your pickles a depth and warmth that are perfect for fall or winter vegetables. If you prefer a spicy kick, chili flakes or whole dried chilies will add that heat, making your pickles stand out with a fiery bite.

Adding bay leaves brings a deeper, herbal undertone to the brine, enhancing the overall complexity of the flavor. For a more aromatic touch, garlic, shallots, or onions can be added, infusing the pickles with savory richness. These ingredients help create pickles that feel heartier and more flavorful, perfect for pairing with sandwiches or as a snack.

Herbs like thyme, rosemary, or tarragon can introduce an elegant, fragrant note to your pickles, lending a light, fresh touch that pairs wonderfully with cucumbers, carrots, or even beans. For a zesty, bright flavor, a bit of citrus zest, like lemon or orange, can add a refreshing tang to your pickles. This is particularly delightful with pickled fruits or lighter vegetables such as radishes.

When customizing your brine, it's essential to maintain a balance. The vinegar's acidity should complement the spices you've chosen, without overpowering them. Always taste your brine before pouring it over the vegetables to ensure the flavors are balanced and harmonious. If you prefer your pickles on the sweeter side, you can adjust the sugar content, or if you like more acidity, you can increase the vinegar slightly.

The beauty of personalizing your pickles lies in the endless possibilities. Whether you enjoy a classic dill pickle with just a hint of garlic, or something more adventurous with a spicy chili and citrus kick, the options are limitless. Experimenting with different spice combinations allows you to tailor your pickles to suit any meal or flavor preference, and over time, you'll perfect a signature blend that's entirely your own.

The key to successful pickling lies in tasting as you go. Trust your instincts, and don't be afraid to try new spice combinations. Each batch of pickles is an opportunity to discover something new and exciting, and with a little experimentation, you'll be able to create unique pickles that elevate your meals and offer a fresh twist on the classic.

Artisan Pickles: Experiment with Different Vegetables and Spices

Artisan pickles go beyond the typical store-bought variety, offering a more creative and personalized way to preserve vegetables. These pickles are all about experimenting with different vegetables, fruits, spices, and brines to create unique, flavorful jars that reflect your personal taste. While cucumbers are often the go-to choice for pickling, you can pickle virtually any vegetable from sweet bell peppers to earthy beets, crunchy cauliflower, or even delicate asparagus.

The key to making artisan pickles is to balance the acidity and spice of the brine with the natural flavors of your ingredients. Whether you prefer spicy pickles or ones with a subtle sweetness, the possibilities are endless. This section will guide you through a variety of pickling recipes using both common and more unusual vegetables, allowing you to create vibrant, flavorful additions to your meals. These pickles are perfect for snacking, adding to charcuterie boards, or enhancing your favorite dishes with a tangy bite.

Let's dive into some creative recipes that will inspire you to experiment and craft your own signature pickles.

Pickled Peppers

Pickled peppers bring a vibrant and tangy crunch to any dish, adding a punch of flavor whether you're serving them as a snack, topping off sandwiches, or as a side to your favorite meals. This recipe combines red, green, and yellow bell peppers, creating a colorful jar that's as pleasing to the eye as it is to the palate. The mustard seed and allspice add warmth and depth to the brine, while the vinegar and sugar balance out the heat with a touch of sweetness.

Ingredients:

- 2-1/2 cups white vinegar
- 1/2 cup sugar
- 6 red bell peppers, sliced
- 6 green bell peppers, sliced
- 6 yellow bell peppers, sliced
- 2 teaspoons pickling salt
- 2 teaspoons mustard seed
- 2 teaspoons whole allspice

Instructions:

Bring the vinegar, sugar, and 2-1/2 cups of water to a boil. Add the peppers and heat through. Remove the peppers from the liquid with a slotted spoon and pack them into sterilized jars. Add 1/2 teaspoon salt, 1/2 teaspoon mustard seeds, and 1/2 teaspoon whole allspice to each jar. Pour the hot liquid over the peppers, leaving 1/4-inch of headspace. Seal and process for 5 minutes once the water starts to boil.

Green Tomato Pickles

This recipe is an excellent way to preserve end-of-season green tomatoes. With the tang of apple cider vinegar and the warmth of spices like cinnamon and cloves, green tomato pickles are a must-have for any pickle lover looking to experiment with different textures and flavors. The result is a slightly sweet, tangy pickle with an aromatic, spicy finish.

Ingredients:

- 5 pounds green tomatoes
- 1/2 cup pickling salt
- 6 onions, sliced
- 3 red bell peppers
- 1/2 cup sugar
- 1/2 tablespoon ground allspice
- 1/2 tablespoon ground cinnamon
- 1/2 tablespoon ground mustard
- 1/2 teaspoon ground cloves
- Apple-cider vinegar

Instructions:

Slice the tomatoes, sprinkle with the salt, and let them sit overnight. In the morning, drain off the liquid. Combine the tomatoes, onions, peppers, sugar, and spices in a large pot. Cover with cider vinegar and bring to a boil. Cook until the vegetables are tender. Pour the mixture into sterilized jars, leaving 1/2-inch of headspace. Seal and process for 10 minutes once the water starts to boil.

Mustard Pickles

Mustard pickles are a colorful, flavorful addition to your pickling repertoire. This recipe features cucumbers, green tomatoes, cauliflower, and bell peppers, all packed into a tangy, mustard-infused brine. The combination of spices, from turmeric to cinnamon, gives these pickles a warm, zesty flavor that will complement a wide variety of dishes.

Ingredients:

- 2 cups pickling salt
- 1 quart sliced cucumbers
- 2 quarts sliced green tomatoes
- 1 quart small button onions
- 1 head cauliflower, broken into small pieces
- 4 green bell peppers, sliced
- 4 red bell peppers, sliced
- 1 bunch celery, finely chopped
- 1-1/2 cups brown sugar
- 1/2 cup all-purpose flour
- 4 tablespoons ground mustard
- 1 teaspoon turmeric
- 2 quarts white vinegar
- 2 sticks cinnamon
- Several whole cloves, to taste

Instructions:

Make a brine by combining 4 quarts of water with the salt, then bring to a boil and add the vegetables. Remove from heat and let sit overnight. Heat the vegetables again in brine, then drain. Mix the brown sugar, flour, mustard, and turmeric with enough cold water to make a smooth paste. Heat the vinegar, add the flour mixture, and cook, stirring often, until smooth. Add the vegetables, cinnamon, and cloves and allow to scald thoroughly. Pour into sterilized jars, leaving 1/4-inch of headspace. Seal and process for 10 minutes once the water starts to boil.

Zucchini Pickles

Zucchini is often in abundance during the summer months, and if you're looking for a way to preserve it for later, pickling is the perfect solution. These Zucchini Pickles are crunchy, tangy, and spiced with mustard seeds, celery seed, and turmeric for a flavorful, savory bite. They're a great way to make use of the surplus zucchini from your garden or farmer's market, and they're the perfect accompaniment to sandwiches, salads, or as a snack on their own.

Ingredients:

- 2 quarts thinly sliced, unpeeled zucchini
- 2 onions, thinly sliced
- 1/4 cup pickling salt
- 2 cups white vinegar
- 2 cups sugar
- 2 teaspoons mustard seed
- 1 teaspoon celery seed
- 1 teaspoon turmeric

Instructions:

Begin by placing the zucchini and onions in a bowl, sprinkling them with the pickling salt, and covering them with cold water. Let them stand for 2 hours, then drain and rinse with fresh water before draining again. In a pot, combine the vinegar, sugar, mustard seed, celery seed, and turmeric, and bring it to a boil, cooking for 2 minutes. Add the zucchini and onions to the brine, remove from heat, and let it sit for 2 hours. Afterward, bring the mixture back to a boil and cook for an additional 5 minutes. Pour the hot mixture into sterilized jars, leaving 1/4-inch of headspace. Seal the jars and process them for 10 minutes in a boiling-water canner, starting when the water begins to boil.

Pickled Asparagus: A Delicate, Tangy Delight

Pickled asparagus is a true treat, offering a crisp, tangy bite that complements everything from charcuterie boards to simple salads. Asparagus is particularly well-suited to pickling because it holds up beautifully, absorbing the brine while maintaining its structure. This Pickled Asparagus recipe combines garlic, hot peppers, and dill seed to add savory depth and a little spice, making it a versatile addition to your pickle collection.

Ingredients:

- 10 lbs asparagus
- 6 large garlic cloves
- 4-1/2 cups water
- 4-1/2 cups white distilled vinegar (5%)
- 6 small hot peppers (optional)
- 1/2 cup canning salt
- 3 teaspoons dill seed

Instructions:

Wash the asparagus thoroughly and trim the stems so that they fit into your canning jar, leaving about 1/2-inch of headspace at the top. Place one garlic clove at the bottom of each jar and tightly pack the asparagus with the tips facing down. In a large pot, bring the water, vinegar, hot peppers (optional), salt, and dill seed to a boil. Once boiling, pour the brine over the asparagus in the jars, leaving 1/2-inch of headspace. Remove air bubbles, adjust the headspace if needed, and wipe the rims of the jars with a damp paper towel. Seal the jars and process in a boiling-water canner for 10 minutes for pints or 15 minutes for quarts, depending on your altitude.

Fruit Pickles: Sweet, Tangy, and Unexpectedly Delicious

Fruit pickles are a delightful twist on traditional pickling, transforming fresh fruits into tangy, flavorful preserves. While pickling is typically associated with vegetables, fruits like peaches, pears, and watermelon can be pickled to create sweet, tangy, and slightly spiced treats. These pickles are perfect for adding a unique touch to your meals or enjoying on their own as a snack. Whether you prefer a sweet pickled peach or a spiced watermelon pickle, the possibilities are endless.

This section will guide you through various fruit-based pickling recipes that blend sweetness, acidity, and spices to create vibrant, one-of-a-kind preserves.

Sweet Pickled Peaches: A Tangy and Sweet Summer Treat

These Sweet Pickled Peaches are the perfect balance of tangy and sweet, offering a unique and delightful way to preserve peaches. The cinnamon, cloves, and vinegar work harmoniously to create a rich and aromatic brine that complements the natural sweetness of the peaches. Let them ferment for a few weeks, and you'll have a deliciously spiced treat that's perfect for snacking or pairing with cheese.

Ingredients:

- 8 to 10 small, firm, ripe peaches
- Whole cloves
- 2 cups white vinegar
- 2 cups sugar
- 2 cinnamon sticks (3-inch)

Instructions:

Start by scalding the peachesplace them in boiling water for a few minutes, then transfer them to an ice-water bath to stop the cooking process. Peel the skins off, keeping the peaches whole (don't stone them), and insert 3 cloves into each peach. In an enamel pot, combine the vinegar, sugar, 6 cloves, cinnamon sticks, and 1 cup of water. Bring to a boil, then cover and let it boil for 5 minutes.

Carefully add the peaches, a few at a time, into the boiling brine and continue to cook until the peaches are tender. Once they're soft, spoon the peaches into sterilized jars and pour the hot liquid over the peaches, leaving 1/2 inch of headspace. Seal the jars and process for 20 minutes in a boiling-water canner, starting when the water begins to boil.

Watermelon Pickles: A Sweet and Savory Summer Surprise

Watermelon Pickles are a surprising and delightful way to use watermelon rind. With the perfect balance of sweet, tangy, and aromatic spices, these pickles will add a unique twist to your summer pickle repertoire. The rind transforms into a crunchy, slightly sweet treat that pairs beautifully with cheese, sandwiches, or simply as a snack.

Ingredients:

- Rind from half of a large watermelon
- 6 cups sugar
- 1 pint apple-cider vinegar
- 1 tablespoon whole cloves
- 1 tablespoon whole allspice
- 1 cinnamon stick, broken

Instructions:

Start by slicing the watermelon rind into 1-inch strips, then carefully peel off the green skin. Cut the rind into 1-inch chunks and cover with cold water in a pot. Boil for 20 minutes, then drain. In a separate pot, combine the sugar and vinegar. Tie the cloves, allspice, and cinnamon stick in a cheesecloth bag and add it to the vinegar and sugar mixture. Bring the brine to a boil and pour it over the watermelon rind.

Cover the jar and allow the rind to sit overnight. The next day, drain the rind but reserve the liquid and spices. Bring the brine to a boil again and pour it over the rind, allowing it to sit overnight a second time.

Finally, bring the rind and brine to a boil together until the rind becomes translucent and the liquid thickens to a honey-like consistency. Pack the rind into sterilized jars and pour the hot brine over it, leaving 1/2-inch of headspace. Seal and process the jars for 5 minutes in a boiling-water canner, starting when the water begins to boil.

Homemade Vinegar: Crafting Your Own Flavors

Vinegar is one of the essential ingredients in many pickling and fermenting processes. Why not take it a step further by crafting your own homemade vinegar? Making vinegar at home allows you to control the flavor and quality, and it's easier than you might think. You can create vinegars from almost any fruit, herb, or spice, allowing for a completely customized product that can be used in cooking, salad dressings, or as a base for pickling.

Basic Homemade Vinegar Recipe:

Ingredients:

- cups fruit juice (such as apple, grape, or berry juice) or wine
- 1/4 cup sugar
- 1 tablespoon raw vinegar (this acts as the starter culture)

Instructions:

To begin making homemade vinegar, pour your chosen fruit juice or wine (such as apple, grape, or berry juice) into a clean glass jar. Add sugar to the jar and stir well until it dissolves completely, ensuring the mixture is evenly sweetened. Next, introduce 1 tablespoon of raw vinegar to the jar; this will serve as your starter culture, providing the bacteria necessary for the fermentation process.

Cover the jar with a clean cloth and secure it with a rubber band or string. This allows air to flow into the jar while keeping out any dust or contaminants. Place the jar in a warm, dark spot with a temperature of about 70°F (21°C). Stir the vinegar every few days, checking for signs of fermentation, such as bubbles or slight changes in scent. After 2–3 weeks, taste the vinegar; once it reaches the acidity level you desire, strain it to remove any solids and transfer it to a sealed jar for storage. If you prefer a stronger, more acidic vinegar, let it ferment for an additional few weeks before straining and storing.

Flavoring Your Vinegar:

Once you have your base vinegar, you can infuse it with herbs, spices, or fruits to create custom-flavored vinegars. Try adding rosemary and garlic for a savory vinegar, citrus zest for a refreshing twist, or chili peppers for a spicy kick. The key is to experiment and create a vinegar that reflects your taste.

Fermented Condiments: Mustard, Mayonnaise, and More

Fermented condiments add a tangy depth of flavor to your meals, and they're easier to make than you might think. Homemade mustard, mayonnaise, and ketchup can be customized with your favorite flavors, and fermenting them adds a probiotic boost.

Fermented Mustard:

Making mustard from scratch is simple and offers endless possibilities. Combine mustard seeds with water, vinegar, salt, and optional spices like turmeric, garlic, or herbs. Allow the mustard to ferment for a few days, then blend it into your desired consistency.

Fermented Mayonnaise:

For fermented mayonnaise, combine egg yolks, mustard, vinegar, and oil, and let the mixture ferment at room temperature for a couple of days. This gives the mayonnaise a tangy, probiotic kick that's perfect for sandwiches or as a dip.

How to Make Wild Ferments: A Guide to Spontaneous Fermentation

Wild fermentation is the art of allowing naturally occurring microorganisms, present in the air and on the ingredients themselves, to ferment your food. Unlike cultured ferments, where specific bacteria are added, wild fermentation relies on the natural bacteria and yeasts in your environment. This process can result in unique and complex flavors, but it requires patience and a bit of luck.

To make wild ferments, you need high-quality, organic ingredients that haven't been treated with pesticides or chemicals, as these can hinder the fermentation process. Start with simple vegetables like cabbage, carrots, or radishes, and avoid using salt or vinegar initially. Instead, let the natural bacteria on the vegetables do the work.

Once the fermentation begins, you'll notice changes in the color, texture, and flavor of the vegetables. Wild ferments can be unpredictable, but this is part of the fun! They often take longer than cultured ferments, so be patient and check on them regularly.

This chapter has taken you beyond the basics of fermentation, allowing you to experiment with creating personalized flavors and signature preserves. By crafting your own custom spice blends for pickles, making homemade vinegars, experimenting with fermented condiments, and exploring wild fermentation, you can truly make your preserves unique. The world of fermentation is vast, and each batch offers a new opportunity to learn and improve. As you advance in your fermentation skills, remember that the key is creativity so don't hesitate to try new combinations and flavors to make each ferment your own. The journey of crafting your signature preserves is just beginning!

Conclusion

The Joy of Pickling and Fermenting - A Journey to Flavor and Wellness

As you close this book and reflect on the techniques, recipes, and insights you've gained, remember that pickling and fermenting are not just about preserving food. They are about embracing the rich history of food preservation, understanding the profound benefits of fermentation, and creating flavors that speak to the heart of homegrown, homemade nourishment. These ancient techniques have been passed down through generations, and now, as you embark on your own journey, you are becoming part of that time-honored tradition of preserving nature's bounty.

Pickling and fermenting allow you to transform simple ingredients into vibrant, flavorful, and nutrient-rich foods. Whether you're creating tangy pickles, probiotic-packed fermented vegetables, or experimenting with fruit-based preserves, you're opening a world of culinary possibilities. The versatility of pickling and fermenting means that there is no limit to what you can create whether it's a classic jar of dill pickles or an adventurous batch of spicy kimchi, the possibilities are endless.

But beyond the flavors and textures that come with these foods, pickling and fermenting also offer incredible health benefits. Fermented foods, rich in probiotics, provide your gut with beneficial bacteria that can support digestion, boost your immune system, and even promote mental wellness. The process of fermentation enhances the bioavailability of nutrients, making them easier for your body to absorb and benefiting your overall health. Pickled foods, on the other hand, provide vitamins, minerals, and antioxidants that nourish your body, all while offering a satisfying and tangy crunch.

As you experiment with the techniques you've learned, remember that patience is key. The magic of fermentation and pickling doesn't happen overnight, but it's worth the wait. Whether you're working with cucumbers, cabbage, carrots, or even more adventurous ingredients like watermelon rind or garlic, each batch brings you closer to mastering the art of food preservation. And along the way, you'll create foods that reflect your personal tastes, preferences, and creativity.

But the benefits of this practice go beyond just the food itself. By pickling and fermenting at home, you're taking control of what you eat and how it's made. You can choose the freshest ingredients, adjust the flavor profiles to suit your tastes, and avoid the preservatives and additives found in store-bought versions. There's a deep sense of satisfaction in knowing that the jars lining your pantry are filled with foods you made yourself, foods that are as nourishing as they are flavorful.

Moreover, pickling and fermenting foster a sense of connection to the seasons and to the food we grow. It's a way to capture the essence of summer's bounty and enjoy it throughout the year. Whether you're preserving an abundant harvest from your garden or buying fresh produce at your local farmers' market, these techniques allow you to savor the flavors of the season at any time. And in a world where so much food is mass-produced and disconnected from its origins, the process of pickling and fermenting brings us back to something more authenticsomething that connects us to nature and to the people we share our meals with.

As you continue to explore the world of pickling and fermenting, don't be afraid to experiment and try new things. Add more spices, change the sugar-to-vinegar ratio, or throw in a new vegetable or fruit you've never worked with before. There's no right or wrong way to pickle and ferment only the method that works best for you. And as you grow more confident in your skills, you'll find that the act of creating these foods becomes a joyous part of your routine, a tradition that you can pass down to others.

So, as you seal your jars and store them away, know that you are preserving much more than just food. You are preserving a piece of history, a piece of culture, and a piece of your own creativity. You are embracing the art of food preservation, not just for the flavors and health benefits it provides, but for the joy it brings to the kitchen and to the people you share your creations with.

In the end, pickling and fermenting is about more than just food. It's about connection, tradition, health, and creativity. It's about taking the time to slow down and enjoy the process of making something from scratch. And most importantly, it's about sharing the fruits of your labor with others and savoring the joy of food that's made with care, love, and a touch of patience.

So, keep experimenting, keep learning, and most of all, keep enjoying the wonderful world of pickling and fermenting. Your journey to flavor and wellness has just begun, and there's a whole world of possibilities waiting for you in every jar.